Nada but EMPaNaDaS

History and Recipes

Marina Arbetman-Rabinowitz
and Linda Kern Hayon

ISBN-13: 978-1484072608
ISBN-10:148407260X

Library of Congress Control Number: 2013907320
CreateSpace Independent Publishing Platform
North Charleston, South Carolina

DEDICATION

For Ian, Hannah, and Josh who have been putting up with me,
and my cooking, for over 25 years.
In honor of my roots; good or bad they are mine.
En honor a mis raíces; buenas o malas son las mías.

For my children: Oren, Ronni, Julie, and Kathleen.
And for my beloved grandchildren—my little *empanaditas.*
And in memory of Yehiel, who would be so proud.

THANKS

The genesis for this book developed out of life crises and a deep friendship. After years of laughing, traveling and crying together, we realized that the best and most meaningful conversations occurred when we were planning menus and cooking with and for friends.

One of the many trips we took together was to Argentina where Marina hoped to share some of her childhood memories with Linda. Of course, it took only two bites of Buenos Aires' amazing variety of empanadas before Linda was ready to adopt the country and its cuisine as her own. We continued to explore Buenos Aires and then Patagonia in search of the very best empanada. Upon reflection, instead of moving to Argentina, the two of us decided to bring the iconic food back home. After a great deal of cooking, research and tasting we opened a small business in New Mexico called Nada but Empanadas.

Along the road many people contributed to our success. We owe them a great deal and we would like to acknowledge them here. To start with, creating this book required writing, tweaking, testing and retesting every recipe. Our empanadas even flew long distance to be tasted. Thanks to Hannah, Ronni, Kathleen, Oren, Julie and the Lang- Suskin family. Special thanks to our taster-in-chief: Josh.

Our thanks to Phil Kaplan for helping us with the initial business plan and giving us valuable marketing ideas. Phil also played the role of our food photographer, and always strived to capture the empanadas' best profile in his shots. (The handmade ceramic serving pieces pictured are courtesy of the authors.)

Many other friends supported us and gave us excellent advice. Havi Graeber encouraged us

to get started. Terry Revo helped us navigate the legal maze. Thanks to all our clients who believed in us from the beginning, including Dinorah Gutierrez, Marie Baca, Cheri Goldman, Diana Cortez, Marti Revo, Marlies Diels, Terri Berrenberg, Rosanne Kaplan, Helen Horwitz, Kris Cannaday, Shelley Koffler, and Helen Cortina-Weiss of NBC Latino. Thanks also to Sharon Levin from Gourmet to Go. Leah Sandman, of Leah Sandman Design, assisted us in the design of our logo and web page. Aaron Rosenstein from Amazon and Seth Gardenswartz gave us helpful advice on publishing.

Indeed "it takes a village" and we are so grateful to all our empanada-loving villagers!

M.A.R and L.K.H

CONTENTS

INTRODUCTION

Empanadas have had a presence in many cultures since ancient times and today one can find empanadas (or variations thereof) in all corners of the world. They are the perfect choice for lunch or dinner accompanied by soup or salad. They are convenient and portable for school and work lunches. They are elegant and unique when served as appetizers at any cocktail party. They can be made in advance and frozen until ready to bake, or they can be made while chatting with friends as the party gets started. Get ready to fall in love with these handheld treats!

Historical Travels of the Empanada

The concept of what we know now as empanadas is not new. In fact, the name "empanada" (which translates as "inside" or "between bread") did not come to be until this dish arrived in Spain centuries ago.

The first accounts date back to the year 2500 BCE in Persia, where due to the warm climate and the nomadic way of living, people needed a way to preserve their food. The idea of putting filling in between what probably was a stale roll aided in not only giving flavor and moisture to an otherwise inedible piece of bread, but also in protecting the inside filling from the elements and making food easily portable. What genius: no need for plates or flatware, minimal mess, and maximum shelf life!

Greece was another birthplace of dough (*phyllo*) that found its way to Armenia, Morocco, and the Middle East. However, the major significant journey of the empanadas seems to have occurred around the year 700 CE. Tariq, an Algerian military officer, was dispatched to occupy Tangier, north of Morocco, and from there to make his way to Spain. The story is that Tariq brought many of his Algerian cultural influences to Spain, the empanada among them. Of course, there is also the theory that the empanada traveled to Spain via Italy, where they were known as *calzone*. But without a doubt, the empanada made its home in Spain, especially in Asturias and Galicia. The fact that there are images of the dish in paintings and sculptures as early as the twelfth century is a sign of the early success of this kind of food in Spain. For example, a famous sculptor from that century, Maestro Mateo, depicted an empanada in a sculpture located in the portal of the Cathedral of Santiago de Compostela!

In the U.K., the Cornish pasty is a national dish. The travels of the pasty to England are not well known, but old documents from the XII century show that King Henry III partook of pasties and they were a food of the wealthy and upper classes. The word pasty seems to have had its origins in medieval French: *pasté*. Pasties became prevalent in the XVII and XVIII centuries. At that time, the pasty was the typical lunch for working coal miners. Their wives would make large pasties containing two sections of filling: main course and dessert. In one of the corners of the folded pasty, the edge closest to the sweet filling, the dough was significantly thicker and served the purpose of being the "handle". After eating the pasty, the miners often discarded that piece of thick dough since it was grimy with coal dust. Later on, it was proven that throwing away the "handle" was a wise health decision.

Starting around the year 1200, but especially after Columbus' voyage, it was the Spanish conquerors who during their travels, brought Christianity, the Spanish language, and the empanada to Central and South America. This delicious dish spread through every corner of the continent and each country/ province made their own versions. Latin American countries have ongoing competitions and friendly but highly partisan disputes over who makes the most flavorful empanadas. Each region has incorporated local ingredients, flavors, and cooking methods.

Empanadas from around the World

Nearly every culture has a version of empanadas, whether they are fried or baked, filled with sweet or savory fillings, created in different sizes and shapes, or made with a variety of different dough recipes. In the United States they are called turnovers or hand pies. Empanadas in Spain are the size of a pie or of a large rectangle which is then cut into portions; empanadas in Latin America are the same size as *empanadillas* in Spain. The famous *empanada Gallega* is filled with tuna and other vegetables and is an important dish eaten during Lent in Catholic countries. In Italy they are significantly larger than *empanadillas,* are filled with mozzarella and variety of Mediterranean ingredients, and are called *calzone.* You will find Cornish pasties in the U.K. and *spanakopita* in Greece. In Israel you order *borekas* or *knishes*, while in Lebanon and Syria they are known as *fatay* or *sphiha*. In Asia, one can find versions in Mongolia (*khuushuur*), in Russia and Poland (*piroshky*), in India (*samosas*), and in Afghanistan (*bolani*). Jamaicans have their sweet and spicy beef patties. Even within Latin America, different countries have regionally specific takes on empanadas, such as *llaucha* or *pukacapa* in Bolivia, *pastel* in Brazil, *arepas* or *pandebono* in Columbia. In Mexico, sweet empanadas are often eaten for breakfast or dessert. Favorites include pumpkin, yams, fruit, sweet cheese and cream. The empanada dough is usually made with wheat flour, but occasionally it is made with yucca flour.

An influx to the U.S. of Asians, Latin Americans, and other immigrants during the 1960s raised the profile of their hand-held lunch and dinner staples, and many people (including the authors) have fallen in love with these little portable pockets of goodness. What's not to love? They are quick and tasty, crisp and golden on the outside, filled with something delicious inside, perfect for any time of day, and delicious hot or at room temperature.

In this book, we have chosen to focus on South American empanadas—specifically Argentinean. (We have taken the liberty, however, of including recipes for sweet dessert empanadas, which are not typical in that area.) We researched and tested and ate empanadas for over a year, which led to the start of our small business in New Mexico. Now we are ready to share our recipes and our love for these pockets of deliciousness with you. *¡Buen Provecho!*—and enjoy.

CHAPTER 1

Empanada Dough

Making your own empanada dough takes a bit of patience and practice, but it is not difficult. The unit yield in the recipes is calculated using a 4½- to 5½- inch round cookie cutter, which is the average size in Latin America. A 4½-inch round cookie cutter is usually more widely available in many stores, although an extensive variety of sizes is available online.

Pointers for Savory Dough

- The ratio of butter to shortening can be altered. More shortening creates flakier dough; more butter enhances the rich flavor.

- If you want to fry rather than bake your empanadas, butter should not be used; all the fat should be vegetable shortening or lard.

- The dough may be refrigerated and wrapped in plastic for up to three days but at least for two hours before rolling.

- The dough may be frozen in a ball or in round disks, well wrapped, ready to be used after defrosting. Thaw overnight in the refrigerator before using. The dough in a ball can be frozen for up to two months. If the disks are already cut, they may be frozen for up to a month; after that the edges of the disks tend to dry. Remember to defrost the dough overnight in the refrigerator before assembling.

- *Note:*
  2- to 3½-inch disks are commonly used for small appetizer empanadas

  4½- to 5½-inch disks are regular size (common in South America)

  6- to 8-inch disks are used for large empanadas

Traditional Empanada Dough
Makes 24 empanadas

This recipe is adapted from Francis Mallman's recipe for empanada dough in *Seven Fires* (Workman Publishing Company: 2009).

  1½ cups water

  1 tablespoon kosher salt

  3 tablespoons vegetable shortening

  1 to 1½ teaspoons of any dry herb that complements the filling such as paprika, cumin, dill, or parsley

  1 teaspoon vegetable oil or olive oil

  4½ to 5 cups all-purpose flour (plus extra for rolling out dough)

Bring the water and salt to a rolling boil in a small saucepan over medium-high heat. Meanwhile, in a small bowl, mix the dry herb and the oil together with a fork until blended. Remove the saucepan from the heat and add the shortening and the herb/oil mixture. Stir until the shortening is melted. Cool until the mixture is lukewarm and then transfer to a large shallow mixing bowl. Add the flour, a cup at a time mixing with a fork. Once the flour is absorbed, begin mixing the dough with your hands until it gathers itself into a ball. Turn the dough out on a surface sprinkled with flour. Knead until the dough is smooth and elastic, about five minutes. The dough will feel dry. Gather it into a ball and cover well with plastic wrap and refrigerate for at least three hours or overnight before using.

When you are ready to make empanadas, remove the dough from the refrigerator and on a floured surface, roll out the portion of dough until it is about ⅛ -inch thick or less. Using a 4½- to 5½-inch round cookie cutter, or using a saucer as a template, cut out disks of dough. Scraps of dough may be gathered up and re-rolled.

Continue rolling and cutting the dough, stacking the prepared disks between pieces of waxed paper or plastic wrap to prevent them from sticking together or drying out. They are then ready to be filled (see Chapters III to V), folded, crimped, brushed, and baked (see Chapter II).

Baked Empanada Dough
Makes 24 empanadas

> 3 cups all-purpose flour
>
> ¾ tablespoon salt
>
> 2 tablespoons dry parsley **or** 1 tablespoon of any dry herb that complements the filling such as paprika, cumin, or dill
>
> 4 tablespoons (½ stick) cold unsalted butter, cut into cubes
>
> 4 tablespoons vegetable shortening or lard
>
> ¾ to 1 cup ice water

Add the flour, salt, and herbs in a large bowl and whisk to combine. Add the butter and the shortening and mix into the flour using a pastry cutter (or two forks). It is better not to use your hands for mixing because the warmth of your hands will soften the butter. When the mix resembles coarse cornmeal, start incorporating the water until the dough forms a ball. This is the time to mix with your hands. If needed, add more water or more flour. It is better to have slightly dry dough than one that is too wet. After kneading 5 to 7 times, gather the dough into a ball, wrap in plastic wrap, and refrigerate for at least three hours or overnight.

When you are ready to make empanadas, remove the dough from the refrigerator and on a floured surface, roll out the dough until it is about $1/8$ inch thick or less. Using a 4½- to 5½-inch-round cookie cutter, or using a saucer as a template, cut out disks of dough. Scraps of dough may be gathered up and re-rolled.

Continue rolling out and cutting the dough, stacking the prepared disks between pieces of waxed paper or plastic wrap to prevent them from sticking together or drying out. They are then ready to be filled (see Chapters III to V), folded, crimped, brushed, and baked (see Chapter II).

Baked Empanada Dough - Option II
Makes 12 (8-inch-diameter) empanadas

This recipe produces a crust that is flakier and richer than the traditional baked empanada dough. It is typically used for Cornish pasties, but works well with any filling.

3¼ cups all-purpose flour

1½ teaspoons kosher salt

1½ teaspoons sugar

¾ teaspoon baking powder

½ pound (2 sticks) cold unsalted butter, cubed

¾ cup ice water

Mix the flour, salt, sugar and baking powder in a large mixing bowl. Cut in the butter with a pastry blender (or two forks) until mixture resembles coarse crumbs. Add the ice water a little at a time, tossing with the forks or pastry blender to make a pastry-like dough. Add a bit more water if it seems dry and doesn't hold together when squeezed lightly. Gather the dough into a ball, press firmly into a disk, wrap in plastic wrap, and chill for 30 minutes to an hour.

When you are ready to make empanadas, remove the dough from the refrigerator and on a floured surface, roll out the dough until it is about ¹/₈ to ¼ inch thick. Using a 8-inch round cookie cutter, or using a saucer as a template, cut out disks of dough. Scraps of dough may be gathered up and re-rolled.

Continue rolling out and cutting the dough, stacking the prepared disks between pieces of waxed paper or plastic wrap to prevent them from sticking together or drying out. They are then ready to be filled (see Chapters III to VI), folded, crimped, brushed, and baked (see Chapter II).

NOTE: Shortening may be substituted for the butter to make dough that is not as rich. This dough may also be made in the food processor.

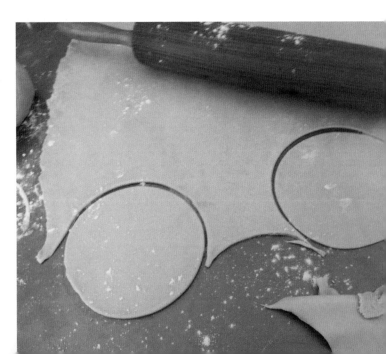

Masa Harina Empanada Dough
Makes 24 empanadas

Masa harina can be found in the Latin American section of many supermarkets.

2½ cups all-purpose flour

½ cup masa harina (finely ground corn flour; do not use corn meal)

1 tablespoon salt

2 tablespoons vegetable shortening or lard

1 cup water

Combine the dry ingredients in a large bowl. Add the shortening and blend together using a pastry cutter or two forks. Gradually incorporate the water until the dough forms a ball. If needed, add more water. Knead the dough a few times, wrap in plastic wrap, and refrigerate at least two hours or overnight.

When you are ready to make empanadas, remove the dough from the refrigerator. On a floured surface, roll out the dough until it is about ⅛ inch thick. Using a 4½- to 5½-inch round cookie cutter, or using a saucer as a template, cut out disks of dough. Scraps of dough may be gathered up and re-rolled.

Continue rolling out and cutting the dough, stacking the prepared disks between pieces of waxed paper or plastic wrap to prevent them from sticking together. They are then ready to be filled (see Chapters III to V), folded, crimped, brushed, and baked (see Chapter II).

NOTE: Empanadas made with masa harina dough are really good fried rather than baked. Just fry in deep fat heated to 350 degrees for 4 to 5 minutes, turning occasionally, until golden brown. Drain on paper towels.

Pointers for Pastry Dough
- *Keep your ingredients as cold as possible before using.*

- *Flakiness comes from cutting the butter into the dry ingredients; for best results, use a pastry blender or two forks to blend. You can use your fingers, but the warmth from your hands may cause the pastry to be tough.*

- *When adding liquids, add them gradually until the dough just comes together when it is gently squeezed. Take care not to over mix or to add too much liquid.*

- *Chilling the dough before rolling out is an important step. When you are ready to make the empanadas, remove the dough from the refrigerator and let it sit at room temperature for 10 to 15 minutes, or until pliable. Keep the unused dough in the refrigerator wrapped in plastic wrap. While cutting out your dough, if it feels too soft or warm, wrap it up and refrigerate it for 5 or 10 minutes before continuing.*

- *When rolling out the dough, use only enough flour to prevent sticking; too much flour will make the dough tough. Roll the dough from the center toward the outside edge, using a heavy rolling pin, lightly floured. The dough should be rolled out until it is approximately ¼ inch thick (thicker than the savory dough) before cutting into circles.*

- *The dough may be frozen in a ball or in round disks for up to two months, well wrapped, ready to be used after defrosting. Thaw overnight in the refrigerator before using.*

- *Note:*
  2- to 3½-inch disks are commonly used for small appetizer empanadas

4½- to 5½-inch disks are considered regular size

Pastry Dough
Makes 16 to 18 empanadas

2¼ cups all-purpose flour, sifted

¾ teaspoon salt

2 tablespoons sugar

½ pound (2 sticks) unsalted butter, very cold, cut into cubes

6 tablespoons ice water

In the bowl of a food processor, combine the flour, sugar, and salt. Pulse a few times to combine. While pulsing, add the cubes of butter (a few at a time), and pulse until the mixture resembles wet sand (about 10 to 15 seconds). With the processor running, add the ice water, one tablespoon at a time, until the dough forms a ball. This should take less than 30 seconds. If the dough is still crumbly, add another half tablespoon of water. Remove the dough from the work bowl. Divide the dough in half, shape each half into a flattened disk, and wrap each half in plastic wrap. Don't knead or overwork the dough—the less you handle it the better, since the heat from your hands will melt the bits of butter that are dispersed through the dough. Refrigerate at least two hours or overnight before rolling out.

When you are ready to make empanadas, remove the dough from the refrigerator. Let it sit at room temperature for 10 minutes. On a floured surface, roll out the dough until it is ¼ inch thick and using a 4- to 4½-inch round cookie cutter, or using a saucer as a template, cut out disks of dough. Scraps of dough may be gathered up and re-rolled to make additional disks.

Continue rolling out and cutting the dough, stacking the prepared disks between pieces of waxed paper or plastic wrap to prevent them from sticking together. They are then ready to be filled (see Chapter VI), folded, crimped, brushed, and baked (see Chapter II).

Variations:
- *Add ½ teaspoon ground cinnamon to the flour*

- *Add 1 teaspoon grated orange or lemon zest to the flour*

- *Replace a portion of the butter with vegetable shortening for extra flakiness*

- *Replace part of the butter with cream cheese*

- *Add an additional tablespoon or two of sugar for a sweeter, crispier baked dessert empanada*

Gluten-free Dough
Makes 12 empanadas

Gluten-free flour is available in health food stores, organic food markets, and many large supermarkets. It is recommended that you use a gluten-free flour blend made up primarily of brown and white rice flours (rather than garbanzo bean flour). This dough is tender and may prove a bit difficult to work with when the temperature in your kitchen is hot. Rolling the dough out between sheets of plastic wrap will make it easier. Try not to over-handle the dough. Do not over-fill the empanadas, as gluten-free dough tends to crack rather than stretch.

8 tablespoons vegetable shortening, chilled

8 tablespoons unsalted butter, cold

2¾ cups gluten-free flour (plus extra for rolling out dough)

1 teaspoon salt

1 teaspoon sugar

⅓ cup plus 1 tablespoon ice water

Cut the cold butter and shortening into ½-inch cubes. In a separate bowl, combine flour, salt, and sugar. Using a pastry blender, cut the butter and shortening into the dry ingredients until peas-sized pieces are formed. Add the ice water gradually until the dough comes together. Use up to 1 tablespoon additional ice water, if needed. Chill in refrigerator.

When you are ready to make empanadas, remove the dough from the refrigerator. Let it sit at room temperature for 5 minutes. Between two sheets of plastic wrap sprinkled lightly with gluten-free flour, roll out the dough until it is ¼ inch thick. Using a 4- to 4½-inch round cookie cutter (or using a saucer as a template), cut out disks of dough. Scraps of dough may be gathered up and re-rolled to make additional disks.

Continue rolling out and cutting the dough, stacking the prepared disks between pieces of waxed paper or plastic wrap to prevent them from sticking together. They are then ready to be filled (see Chapters II to VI), folded, crimped, brushed, and baked (see Chapter II). You can adapt the filling recipes to make them gluten-free by substituting flour with cornstarch or potato starch mixed with water.

Shortcuts

If you are short on time, the following ready-made products are perfectly acceptable in place of handmade empanada dough: frozen puff pastry, refrigerated biscuit dough, refrigerated pie dough, refrigerated crescent rolls, wonton skins or egg roll wrappers for fried empanadas, prepared pizza dough, or store-bought empanada disks.

Frozen Puff Pastry

Frozen puff pastry can be found in the freezer case of your supermarket. It can be used for either sweet or savory empanadas. Thaw the package of puff pastry overnight in the refrigerator or at room temperature for an hour. (Thawed puff pastry can be kept refrigerated for up to a week.) When ready to use, carefully unfold and roll out the puff pastry dough on a well-floured surface. (Do not re-roll scraps; the dough will be too heavy.) You should be able to cut 18 3- to 3½-inch small disks from the two sheets of puff pastry in a 17.25 oz. box. Place two teaspoons of the desired filling (see Chapters III to VI) in the center of each dough round. Brush a bit of egg white or warm water on the edges of each circle to help seal the empanadas. Fold in half to cover the filling and press the edges firmly to seal. You can use a fork to crimp the edges. Brush with egg wash (one egg yolk beaten with a tablespoon of water), and bake on a parchment paper-lined baking sheet in a preheated 400 degree oven for 15 to 20 minutes or until golden brown.

Refrigerated Biscuit Dough

Tubes of ready-made biscuit dough can be found in the refrigerated section of your supermarket. You can use buttermilk or regular biscuit dough to make sweet or savory empanadas. Each 7.5 oz. package of 8 biscuits will make 8 empanadas in no time at all. Separate the biscuit dough into 8 pieces and press or roll each piece to get it as thin as possible, approximately ⅛ inch thick. You should get a 5- or 6-inch round of dough, which will produce large empanadas (no need for a cookie cutter). Fill each round of dough with the desired filling (see Chapters III to V), fold over to enclose the filling, press the edges firmly with your fingers and crimp (see Chapter II), and brush with egg wash (one egg yolk beaten with a tablespoon of water). Bake the empanadas on a greased baking sheet at 400 degrees for 12 to 15 minutes, or until the edges are golden brown. This dough produces empanadas that will get nice and brown in the oven, but the texture will be soft rather than crisp.

NOTE: Biscuit dough is somewhat salty and complements savory fillings best, but can be used for sweet fillings as well.

Refrigerated Pie Dough

Packages of prepared pie dough can be found in the refrigerated or dairy section of the supermarket. You may also be able to find it in the freezer section. One package (16 oz.) of pie dough, which usually contains enough pastry to make two 9-inch pies, will make approximately 16 4- to 4½-inch empanadas. Don't use the frozen pie dough that is already pressed into aluminum foil pie tins—use the packages of rolled or folded pie dough. Keep any unused dough in the refrigerator. Allow the package of dough to sit unopened at room temperature for about 10 minutes to make it easier to work with. Unroll one piece at a time and lay it out on a lightly floured surface. Smooth any cracks or folds with your fingers and roll the dough a bit thinner. Cut the dough into circles and brush the edges with water or egg white. Place desired sweet or savory filling (see Chapters III to VI) in the center of each circle, fold in half, and press firmly to seal (see Chapter II for crimping styles). Place the filled empanadas on a lightly greased or parchment paper-lined baking sheet. Brush with egg wash (one egg yolk beaten with one tablespoon water) and bake in a 375 degree preheated oven for 15 to 18 minutes or until golden brown.

NOTE: Pie dough works equally well with savory or sweet fillings.

Refrigerated Crescent Rolls

Eight-ounce tubes of refrigerated crescent roll dough can be found in the refrigerator section of your supermarket. Unroll the dough and lay out on a floured surface. Pinch the seams of the triangles closed and gently roll the dough with a floured rolling pin to a 10x12-inch rectangle about $\frac{1}{8}$ inch thick. You should be able to get eight 4-inch rounds from each tube of crescent roll dough. Cut the dough into rounds (or leave it as the pre-cut triangles) and brush the edges with water or egg white. Place desired sweet or savory filling (see Chapters III to VI) in the center of each circle, fold in half, and press firmly to seal (see Chapter II for crimping styles). Place the filled empanadas on a lightly greased or parchment paper-lined baking sheet. Brush with egg wash (one egg yolk beaten with one tablespoon water) and bake in a 375 degree preheated oven for 10 to 12 minutes or until golden brown.

NOTE: Crescent roll dough works equally well for sweet or savory fillings.

Wonton Skins or Eggroll Wrappers

Eggroll wrappers or wonton skins can be found in the produce section of your supermarket. They are especially well-suited to savory meat, vegetable, or cheese fillings. They usually come in packages of twenty 6-inch square wrappers. To make empanadas from wonton skins or eggroll wrappers, lay out the wrappers on your counter. Place about 2 teaspoons of your chosen filling (Chapters III to V) into the middle of each wonton. Dampen the outside edges with your finger dipped in warm water or beaten egg white, and fold over into a triangle-shaped turnover. Press the edges to seal, or use a fork to crimp the edges together. (While you are making the empanadas, keep the wrappers covered with a dampened kitchen towel to prevent them from drying out.) Brush the tops of the filled empanadas with a bit of olive or sesame oil. They can be baked on a greased baking sheet for 13 to 15 minutes at 375 degrees, or you can fry them in shallow hot canola oil for about 2 minutes, turning occasionally, until golden brown. Remove with a slotted spoon and drain on paper towels.

NOTE: Wonton or eggroll wrappers work best with savory fillings.

Pizza Dough

Prepared pizza dough can be found in the refrigerated section of your supermarket. You can find it packaged in tubes or wrapped in plastic. Some pizzerias will sell you their pizza dough. You can also find whole wheat pizza dough in some stores. Unwrap the dough and place it on a lightly floured surface. 10 oz. of pizza dough will yield eight to ten 4½-inch disks or twelve to fifteen 3½-inch disks. Roll the dough into a 10x12-inch rectangle, about $\frac{1}{8}$ inch thick. Use a round cookie cutter to cut circles in the dough and brush the edges with water or egg white. Place desired savory filling (Chapters III to V) in the center of each circle, fold in half, and press firmly to seal (see Chapter II for crimping styles). Place the filled empanadas on a lightly greased or parchment paper-lined baking sheet. Brush with egg wash (one egg yolk beaten with a tablespoon of water and bake in a 375 degree preheated oven for 12 to 18 minutes or until golden brown. This dough produces empanadas that will get nice and brown in the oven, but the texture will be soft rather than crisp.

NOTE: Empanadas made with pizza dough resemble Italian calzone; savory fillings work best.

Store-bought Empanada Disks

Prepared empanada disks can be found in the freezer sections of Latin American, Mexican, or international markets. They are usually sold in packages of 10, 12 or 20. You can find disks for frying or for baking. Two brands that you may find are *La Salteña* or *Goya*. Thaw the packages overnight in the refrigerator before using.

CHAPTER II:

Assembling, Crimping Styles, and Baking Empanadas

Pointers for Assembling and Baking

- When assembling your empanadas, gently brush beaten egg white (for sweet empanadas) or warm water (for savory empanadas) around the edge of each circle of dough. This will act as the glue which will help seal the empanada filling inside the dough. Place the desired amount of filling in the center of each dough circle. Fold gently in half to form a half-moon shape and press the edges firmly with your fingers to seal. Use a crimping style (see explanations and pictures shown in this chapter), or the tines of a small fork to completely seal the empanada.

- Brush the tops of the filled empanadas with egg wash (1 egg yolk beaten with 1 tablespoon of water) before placing on the cookie sheet and baking. The egg wash gives your empanadas a beautiful golden brown color when they are baked. Bake the empanadas as directed in the filling recipes.

- If you are not baking your empanadas immediately, do not brush them with egg wash. Simply place all the empanadas on a parchment paper-lined baking sheet, cover loosely with plastic wrap, and refrigerate up to 6 to 8 hours. When ready to bake, remove the plastic wrap, brush with egg wash, and bake as directed.

- If you are freezing unbaked empanadas, place the filled and sealed empanadas on wax or parchment paper on a baking sheet, brush them with egg wash and flash freeze until firm. When frozen, remove them from the baking sheet and place them in an air-tight container with waxed or parchment paper in between layers or in a plastic zip-lock bag. Unbaked empanadas can be frozen for up to 4 months.

- For best results, thaw frozen empanadas overnight in the refrigerator or at room temperature for a couple of hours before baking.

- To bake, simply remove the number of empanadas you need, place them on a baking sheet that has been brushed with a film of vegetable oil and preheated for five minutes (for savory empanadas) or on parchment paper (for sweet ones). You may want to brush with egg wash again for extra shine, and bake the frozen empanadas in a pre-heated oven for a few extra minutes than the recipe calls for, or until golden brown.

- Baking times for savory empanadas are 25 to 30 minutes in a preheated oven at 400 degrees. Baking time for sweet empanadas is 20 to 25 minutes at 375 degrees. Each oven is calibrated slightly differently, so just look for a golden brown crust and the empanadas are ready.

- Baked, cooled empanadas may also be tightly wrapped and frozen. To reheat, thaw in the refrigerator overnight before reheating on a baking sheet in a 325 pre-heated oven for 15 minutes.

1. Traditional rope

2. Scalloped pinch

3. Three folds

4. Peaks

5. Round hat

6. Fork crimping or flat sealing

Crimping Styles *(Repulgues)*

The empanada chef's ultimate personal seal is the crimping style (or *repulgue*). In South American countries you can usually identify the ingredients in the filling by examining the crimping method. In most empanadas stores, the customer is given a "map" of the various crimping styles to know what they are getting. There is one exception: the rope style of *repulgue* is almost always associated with beef empanadas. In the northern part of South America, empanadas are usually closed with no crimping–just by pressing the edges together to seal.

Nada but Empanadas uses unique crimping styles to identify each of the various fillings. Another way to identify the fillings is by adding a complementary herb or spice to the dough (or sprinkle it on top after brushing with egg wash). Various flavors of sweet empanadas can be identified by different colored sugars sprinkled on top. A third way of recognizing the filling is by baking them on the side or vertically (with the seam facing up).

1.   **Traditional rope:**   This crimping style takes a bit of practice but is the most traditional. Before you begin the *repulgue*, the empanada edges have to be tightly pinched and well sealed. It is easiest to leave the sealed empanada on the table as you work to crimp it closed; as you gain confidence, holding the empanada in one hand while crimping with the other is the quickest method. Right-handed people start pleating from bottom to top; left-handed people usually start from the top and work their way down. Make sure the sealed border is wide enough (about ½ inch) to give you plenty of dough to crimp. The thumb and index fingers do most of the work; the rest is wrist movement. Make a first fold, press your two fingers together and continue folding and pressing over the previous fold until there is no more dough to fold.   Fold the last piece over and press it onto itself.

2. **Scalloped pinch:** Start with a half-moon tightly sealed empanada on the work surface or in your hand. The technique is to vertically pinch the dough edge firmly with your thumb and index finger, creating scallops about a half inch apart.   Nada but Empanadas uses this *repulgue* to identify chicken empanadas.

3. **Three folds:** Start with a half-moon tightly sealed empanada on the work surface or in your hand. The technique is to fold the edges in toward the filled area, pressing to seal.   Make three long folds—one on the left

side, one on the right, and then a final one in front. (The final fold will be parallel to the back of the half-moon.) Nada but Empanadas uses this *repulgue* to identify fish or seafood empanadas.

4. Peaks: Start with a half-moon tightly sealed empanada on the work surface or in your hand. The technique is to place your index finger under the sealed edge and pinch the dough underneath it with your middle finger and thumb; a little cylinder will be formed. You can make one in the middle, or two or three. Nada but Empanadas uses this *repulgue* to identify various vegetable empanadas.

5. Round hat: Start with a half-moon tightly sealed empanada on the work surface or in your hand. The technique is to fold the sealed portion upwards and then bring the two ends together and press to seal them. You'll get a round shape like a little hat or a pasta tortel-lini. Nada but Empanadas uses this *repulgue* to identify ham and cheese empanadas.

6. Fork crimping or flat sealing: Start with a half-moon tightly sealed empanada on your work surface and press the edges together firmly to seal. You can leave the edge as is, or use the tines of a small fork to press the edges

together. Press the fork firmly enough to seal, but not so firmly that you break the dough. These two methods are the easiest to master, and they are also recommended when using gluten-free dough or any other tender dough. Nada but Empanadas uses this *repulgue* for sweet fillings and when using gluten-free dough.

Have fun creating your own unique style. Of course, simply crimping the edges closed by pressing firmly with your fingers or the tines of a fork is perfectly fine and gets the job done!

CHAPTER III

Meat and Poultry Fillings

In Latin and Central America, the empanadas are usually prepared with ground beef, wheat flour, and animal fat - but each country, region or province has their own unique variations.

In the north of Argentina (Provinces of Salta and Jujuy) empanadas are quite spicy, due to the addition of red pepper flakes and cayenne. In Salta boiled eggs, scallions, potatoes and tomato paste are added while in Jujuy onions are avoided and green peas included. Boiled eggs and olives are also used in Tucumán and Corrientes. In Córdoba and La Pampa, provinces situated in the middle of the country, empanadas often contain sugar, potatoes and raisins–making them unusual for Argentinean palates that tend to prefer savory, salty foods. Other meats used to make empanadas are lamb, *vizcacha* (a large hare), *yacaré* (cayman) and *mulita* (armadillo).

It would be unfair not to mention some other Latin American countries which also have a strong tradition of empanadas. In Chile, the filling is called "pino" and it has similar ingredients: beef, red pepper flakes, ground cumin, black olives, raisins, boiled eggs and plenty of onion. Bolivia also makes empanadas with pork and rice. Rice filling is also common in the Caribbean, as well as local spices such as cilantro. In Paraguay the beef empanadas are fried and the filling contains rice and bay leaves; the dough is made with warm milk. The empanadas from Uruguay are also fried but they have milder spices and a lower ratio of onions to beef as compared to Chile or Argentina. Peruvians add a lot of yellow peppers and garlic paste, and they mince the beef by hand for their empanadas filling and often use sausage instead of beef. In Brazil, empanadas are also mild and include hard boiled eggs and raisins and sugar as well as bacon. The typical empanada from Ecuador adds cheese to a mild version of the beef filling. Venezuela uses masa harina for the dough and the cooking method is frying; the filling is often made with pork and a bit of red wine. The variations seem marginal but they are very important to each country's national pride and identity!

Argentinean Beef

Makes enough filling for 24 empanadas

½ cup vegetable shortening or lard

1 large (or 2 medium) onion, chopped

1 medium green or red pepper, chopped

1 teaspoon sweet or smoked paprika

1 teaspoon red pepper flakes (or more to taste)

½ tablespoon fresh garlic, chopped

¾ tablespoon salt (or more to taste)

½ teaspoon ground pepper (or more to taste)

1 pound ground beef (15% fat)

1 tablespoon tomato paste or one fresh tomato peeled, seeded and chopped

1 tablespoon dried oregano

1 tablespoon ground cumin

½ cup chopped scallions

1 tablespoon chopped fresh parsley

2 tablespoons raisins or ½ teaspoon sugar (optional)

1 tablespoon red wine vinegar

24 pitted green olives, halved

2 large hard-boiled eggs, coarsely chopped

When ready to assemble and bake you will also need:

1 bowl with salted warm water to seal the empanadas

Egg wash (1 egg yolk beaten with 1 table-spoon water) to brush

Vegetable oil for brushing baking sheet or parchment paper

NOTE: To peel the tomato, submerge it in boiling water for 30 seconds. Remove the tomato with a slotted spoon and put in ice water to cool. The skin will peel off easily.

Heat vegetable shortening or lard in a large pot over medium heat. Add the chopped onions, chopped green pepper, paprika and red pepper flakes. When the onions are transparent and soft (about 10 minutes), turn the heat up and add the garlic, salt and pepper and stir; immediately add the ground beef and tomato. Cook for 5 minutes while stirring, just until the meat is no longer pink. Remove from heat and add the oregano, cumin, scallions and parsley. If you chose to add raisins or sugar they can be added at this time. Let the mixture rest until it is cool. Stir in the vinegar. Leave the filling covered in the refrigerator until the mixture is cold–at least four hours or longer, up to two days.

When ready to make the empanadas, put about 2 to 3 tablespoons of the meat mixture, a piece or two of hardboiled egg and one olive half in the center of a 4½- to 5½- inch dough disk (see Chapter I for dough recipes). Brush half of the edge of the dough with warm water, fold it over the filling, press it with your fingers to seal, and make the *repulgue* (see Chapter II for options). Brush the empanadas with the egg wash.

Brush a baking sheet with a film of canola (or other vegetable oil) and put the sheet in a 400 degree preheated oven. When the oil is hot (about 3 minutes) carefully remove the sheet and place the empanadas on the sheet an inch apart. (Putting the empanadas on a hot oiled baking sheet aids in crisping the base.) Alternatively, you can place the empanadas on a parchment paper-lined baking sheet. Bake for 25 to 30 minutes or until golden brown.

NOTE: Empanadas with this filling can be wrapped well and frozen for future baking, but if adding hard-boiled egg to the filling make sure it is chopped finely or the boiled eggs will loose their chemical integrity.

Chimichurri is sometimes served with beef empanadas (see Chapter VII for a traditional recipe).

Hand-Cut Beef

Makes enough filling for 24 empanadas

1 pound of tri-tip, chuck steak or other marbled cut of beef, trimmed of extra fat, and diced into $1/8$- inch cubes

2 teaspoons salt (or more to taste)

½ teaspoon ground pepper (or more to taste)

½ cup vegetable shortening, lard, or olive oil (divided in ¼ cups)

2 large (or 3 medium) onions, thinly sliced

6 scallions, white and half of the green sliced, divided

1 teaspoon paprika

1 teaspoon red pepper flakes

1 tablespoon minced fresh garlic

1 teaspoon ground cumin

1 tablespoon chopped fresh parsley

2 medium size boiled potatoes, cut into ⅓- inch cubes

2 large hard-boiled eggs, coarsely chopped

When ready to assemble and bake you will also need:

1 bowl with salted warm water to seal the empanadas

Egg wash (1 egg yolk beaten with 1 tablespoon water) to brush

Vegetable oil for brushing baking sheet or parchment paper

Place the cubed beef in a bowl and season with salt and pepper. Meanwhile, heat half the shortening or oil in a large pot over medium heat. Add the chopped onions, the white part of the sliced scallions, paprika and red pepper flakes. When the onions are transparent and soft (10 minutes), turn the heat up and add the garlic and stir. In another pot, heat over high heat the rest of the fat and quickly brown the meat until just seared; immediately add the green part of the sliced scallions and the cumin. Set aside and add the cooked onions mix and the potato cubes. Leave the mix

covered in the refrigerator overnight or longer, up to two days.

When ready to make the empanadas, put about 2 to 3 tablespoons of the meat mixture, a piece or two of hardboiled egg and one olive half in the center of a 4½- to 5½-inch dough disk (see Chapter I for dough recipes). Brush half of the edge of the dough with warm water, fold it over the filling, press it with your fingers to seal, and make the *repulgue* (see Chapter II for options). Brush the empanadas with the egg wash.

Brush a baking sheet with a film of canola (or other vegetable oil) and put the sheet in a 400 degree preheated oven. When the oil is hot (about 3 minutes) carefully remove the sheet and place the empanadas on the sheet an inch apart. (Putting the empanadas on a hot oiled baking sheet aids in crisping the base.) Alternatively, you can place the empanadas on a parchment paper-lined baking sheet. Bake for 25 to 30 minutes or until golden brown.

NOTES: Empanadas with this filling can be wrapped well and frozen for future baking, but if adding hard-boiled egg to the filling make sure it is chopped finely or the boiled eggs will lose their natural texture.

This filling is also very good for fried empanadas (see Chapter II for the best dough for fried empanadas).

Sauces for empanadas are not necessary but they make a great accompaniment.

Chimichurri is sometimes served with beef empanadas (see Chapter VII for a traditional recipe). Black bean dip would also work well.

Chicken Argentinean Style
Makes enough filling for 24 empanadas

¼ cup vegetable shortening

1 large (or 2 medium) onion, chopped

1 teaspoon sweet or smoked paprika

1 medium green pepper, chopped

1 medium red pepper, chopped

1 chicken bouillon cube

2 tablespoons tomato paste or 2 small fresh tomatoes, peeled and chopped

3 cups cooked white and dark chicken cut in cubes, skin removed (rotisserie chicken works well)

½ teaspoon salt (or more to taste)

½ teaspoon ground pepper (or more to taste)

1 teaspoon ground dried oregano

24 green or black olives (halved or whole)

2 large hard-boiled eggs, coarsely chopped (optional)

When ready to assemble and bake you will also need:

1 bowl with salted warm water to seal the empanadas

Egg wash (1 egg yolk beaten with 1 teaspoon water) to brush

Vegetable oil for brushing baking sheet or parchment paper

Heat the shortening in a large pot over medium heat. Add the chopped onions, paprika, green and red pepper, and bouillon cube. When the vegetables are soft (10 minutes), add the tomato paste or tomatoes and stir. Add the cubed chicken, salt, pepper, and oregano. Mix to combine. Leave the chicken filling covered in the refrigerator overnight or longer, up to two days.

When ready to make the empanadas, put about 2 to 3 tablespoons of the chicken mixture, a piece or two of hardboiled egg and one olive half in the center of a 4½- to 5½-inch dough disk (see Chapter I for dough recipes). Brush half of the edge of the dough with warm water, fold it over the filling, press it with your fingers to seal, and make the *repulgue* (see Chapter II for options). Brush the empanadas with the egg wash.

Brush a baking sheet with a film of canola (or other vegetable oil) and put the sheet in a 400 degree preheated oven. When the oil is hot (about 3 minutes) carefully remove the sheet and place the empanadas on the sheet an inch apart.

(Putting the empanadas on a hot oiled baking sheet aids in crisping the base.) Alternatively, you can place the empanadas on a parchment paper-lined cookie sheet. Bake for 25 to 30 minutes or until golden brown.

NOTE: Empanadas with this filling can be wrapped well and frozen for future baking, but if adding hard-boiled egg to the filling make sure it is chopped finely or the boiled eggs will lose their natural texture.

New Mexico Chicken Chile Relleno
Makes enough filling for 24 empanadas

2 tablespoons vegetable or olive oil

1 small yellow onion or half a large onion, chopped

2 cloves garlic, chopped

1 large New Mexico, poblano or Anaheim chile pepper, roasted, peeled and chopped (see directions below)

2 tablespoons unsalted butter

2 tablespoons flour

¾ cup chicken broth

One half of a rotisserie chicken (or ½ of a roasted chicken), skin removed and cut into cubes

½ cup canned (and drained) or frozen corn kernels

²/₃ cup shredded cheese (Cheddar or Monterrey Jack)

Juice of 1 lime

1 teaspoon New Mexico red chile powder or ancho chile powder

½ teaspoon each garlic powder, paprika, dried oregano, and dried cumin

Salt and pepper to taste

When ready to assemble and bake you will also need:

1 bowl with salted warm water to seal the empanadas

Egg wash (1 egg yolk beaten with 1 teaspoon water) to brush

Vegetable oil for brushing baking sheet or parchment paper

To roast the New Mexico, poblano or Anaheim chile pepper, place it on a baking dish under the broiler for 10 minutes, turning a few times, until the skin is blackened, blistered and charred in places. (You can also put the chile pepper directly on the flame of a gas burner for a few minutes, turning it until it is charred.) Place the pepper into a plastic bag and seal; let it steam for five minutes until it is cool enough to handle. The peel should come off easily when rubbed gently with a paper towel. Don't worry if a few pieces of charred skin remain. Remove the stem and seeds of the pepper and chop into pieces. (Alternately, you may use 1 4-oz. can mild or medium roasted chopped green chilies, drained.)

In a skillet over medium heat, warm the oil and add the onions. Sauté for 5 minutes until the onions are soft and translucent. Add the garlic and chopped chile pepper and cook for an additional minute or two. Season with salt and pepper. Remove from heat and put aside.

Over medium heat, melt the butter in a large saucepan. Stir the flour into the melted butter and whisk until a thick paste is formed. Continue cooking and stirring for 1 minute to cook out the floury taste. Slowly add the chicken broth and continue to whisk for 2 to 3 minutes, until the mixture is very thick and creamy. Season with salt and pepper to taste.

Add the cubed chicken, cheese, and corn to the sauce, along with the sautéed veggies and the chile powder, garlic powder, paprika, dried oregano, and dried cumin. Cook for a minute until well combined. Add the lime juice and taste for seasoning. Refrigerate, covered, until cool before assembling empanadas. The filling may be refrigerated covered up to two days.

When ready to make the empanadas, put about 2 to 3 tablespoons of the chicken mixture in the center of a 4½- to 5½-inch dough disk (see Chapter I for dough recipes). Brush half of the edge of the dough with warm water, fold it over the filling, press it with your fingers to seal, and make the *repulgue* (see Chapter II for options). Brush the empanadas with the egg wash.

Brush a baking sheet with a film of canola (or other vegetable oil) and put the sheet in a 400 degree preheated oven. When the oil is hot (about 3 minutes) carefully remove the sheet and place the empanadas on the sheet an inch apart. (Putting the empanadas on a hot oiled baking sheet aids in crisping the base.) Alternatively, you can place the empanadas on a parchment paper lined baking sheet. Bake for 25 to 30 minutes or until golden brown.

NOTE: these empanadas are wonderful served with a side of pico de gallo or salsa.

Turkey

Makes enough filling for 24 empanadas

¼ cup vegetable shortening or olive oil

1 medium onion, chopped

1 medium green pepper, chopped

1 teaspoon sweet or smoked paprika

2 cloves garlic, chopped

1½ pounds ground turkey

2 medium fresh tomatoes, chopped

1 teaspoon salt (or more to taste)

¾ teaspoon ground pepper (or more to taste)

½ teaspoon ground cumin

1 teaspoon dried oregano

1 teaspoon chili powder

1 15-oz. can black beans, drained and rinsed

½ of a 15-oz. can corn, drained and rinsed

2 tablespoons chopped fresh cilantro

½ cup grated mozzarella cheese (optional)

When ready to assemble and bake you will also need:

1 bowl with salted warm water to seal the empanadas

Egg wash (1 egg yolk beaten with 1 teaspoon water) to brush

Vegetable oil for brushing baking sheet or parchment paper

Heat the shortening or olive oil in a large skillet over medium heat. Add the chopped onion, green pepper, and paprika and sauté until softened, about 7 minutes. Add the garlic and cook, stirring for 1 minute. Raise the heat to medium high and add the turkey, breaking it up with a wooden spoon as it browns completely. Add the fresh tomatoes and stir to combine. Add salt, pepper, cumin, oregano, and chili powder. Stir in the black beans and corn and mix to combine, then add the cilantro. Let the mixture cool. Leave the filling covered in the refrigerator overnight or longer, up to two days.

When ready to make the empanadas, put about 2 to 3 tablespoons of the turkey mixture and a generous pinch of grated cheese (if using) in the center of a 4½- to 5½-inch dough disk (see Chapter I for dough recipes). Brush half of the edge of the dough with warm water, fold it over the filling, press it with your fingers to seal, and make the *repulgue* (see Chapter II for options). Brush the empanadas with the egg wash.

Brush a baking sheet with a film of canola (or other vegetable oil) and put the sheet in a 400 degree preheated oven. When the oil is hot (about 3 minutes) carefully remove the sheet and place the empanadas on the sheet an inch apart. (Putting the empanadas on a hot oiled baking sheet aids in crisping the base.) Alternatively, you can place the empanadas on parchment paper-lined baking

sheet. Bake for 25 to 30 minutes or until golden brown.

NOTES: 3 cups of leftover shredded cooked turkey may be used in place of the ground turkey. Just add the turkey to the pan when you add the spices.

For a Middle Eastern flair, add 1 teaspoon of cumin, 1 teaspoon of baharat, and 1 teaspoon of curry powder to the mixture.

***Thanksgiving version:** add diced cooked sweet potatoes to the sautéed vegetables; add ½ teaspoon of ground cinnamon instead of oregano and add an additional ½ teaspoon of cumin.*

Cornish Pasties

Makes enough filling for 18 large pasties (8-inch-round disk)

1 lb. beef chuck shoulder steak or skirt steak

¼ cup butter

2 leeks (white and light green parts), washed well, halved lengthwise, and thinly sliced into half-moons

1 large or 2 small onions, chopped

4 scallions, thinly sliced

1 beef bouillon cube

½ teaspoon dried thyme leaves

1 tablespoon Worcestershire sauce

2 Yukon gold potatoes, peeled, cooked, and cooled

½ cup chopped parsley

salt and pepper to taste

When ready to assemble and bake you will also need:

1 bowl with salted warm water to seal the empanadas

Egg wash (1 egg yolk beaten with 1 teaspoon water) to brush

Vegetable oil for brushing baking sheet or parchment paper

Trim the steak of fat (don't discard the fat), and cut the meat into small, ¼-inch cubes. (Freezing the steak for 15 minutes makes dicing easier.) Melt the butter in a large sauté pan over medium heat, and add the leeks and onions. Cook 2 or 3 minutes until the vegetables are soft, and then add the scallions. Add a piece or two of the reserved beef fat to the pan and allow to melt for a couple of minutes. Remove the fat. Add the beef bouillon cube, thyme, and Worcestershire sauce, and stir to combine. Season with salt and pepper to taste. Raise the heat to medium high and add the beef cubes. Stir and cook until the beef is no longer pink. Remove from heat. Cut the potatoes into cubes just slightly larger than the beef cubes. Add the potatoes and parsley to the pan, and stir to combine. Taste for seasoning; add salt and pepper if needed. Chill the filling for several hours covered in the refrigerator before assembling empanadas.

To make the pasties, put about ¼ cup of the beef filling in the center of a 8-inch dough disk (see Option II dough recipe on page 7). Brush half of the dough edge with warm water, fold it over the filling, press it with your fingers to seal, and make the *repulgue* (see Chapter II for options). Repeat with the remaining filling. Brush the empanadas with egg wash. Make three small slits on the top of the pasty.

Brush a sheet tray with a film of canola (or other vegetable) oil and place in a 400 degree preheated oven. When the oil is hot (about 3 minutes) carefully remove the sheet and place the pasties on the sheet an inch apart. Alternatively, you can place the empanadas

on parchment paper-lined baking sheet. Bake for 10 minutes, take out and put a dot of butter on the slits and then lower the temperature to 375 degrees. Bake for another 30 to 35 minutes or until golden brown.

NOTE: Add cooked chopped carrots and defrosted frozen peas to the filling for a traditional Cornish pasty. Diced cooked turnips or rutabaga are other options.

Ham and Cheese
Makes enough filling for 24 empanadas

1½ cups grated cheese (Swiss, Gruyere, Provolone, or a combination)

2 cups diced, cooked ham

2 tablespoons grated Parmesan cheese

5 scallions, sliced

1 large egg, beaten

1 tablespoon fresh parsley, chopped (optional)

salt and pepper to taste

When ready to assemble and bake you will also need:

1 bowl with salted warm water to seal the empanadas

Egg wash (1 egg yolk beaten with 1 teaspoon water) to brush

Vegetable oil for brushing baking sheet or parchment paper

Mix all the ingredients in a medium size bowl until combined. Set aside.

When ready to make the empanadas put about 2 to 3 tablespoons of the ham and cheese filling in the center of a 4 ½-to 5 ½- inch dough disk (see Chapter I for dough recipes). Brush half of the dough edge with warm water, fold it over the filling, press it with your fingers to seal, then make the *repulgue* (see Chapter II for options). Repeat with the remaining filling. Brush the empanadas with the egg wash.

Brush an oven tray with a film of canola (or other vegetable oil) and put the tray in a 400 degree pre-heated oven. When the oil is hot (around 3 minutes) take the tray out and place the empanadas on the tray an inch apart. (Putting the empanadas on a hot oiled sheet ensures a crispy base.) Alternatively, you can place the empanadas on a parchment paper-lined baking sheet. Bake for 25 to 30 minutes or until golden brown.

CHAPTER IV

Fish and Seafood Fillings

Tuna

Makes enough filling for 24 empanadas

½ cup vegetable shortening or ¼ cup extra virgin olive oil

3 scallions (chopped, white and half of green parts separated)

1 large (or 2 medium) onion, chopped

1 teaspoon sweet or smoked paprika

1 medium green pepper, chopped

1 tablespoon tomato paste

½ cup of canned chopped tomatoes or 2 small fresh tomatoes peeled and chopped

2 8 oz. cans of good quality tuna in water, drained and flaked

½ teaspoon salt (or more to taste)

½ teaspoon ground pepper (or more to taste)

1 teaspoon dried dill or two teaspoons fresh dill, chopped

24 green or black olives (whole or coarsely chopped)

2 large hard-boiled eggs, coarsely chopped (optional)

When ready to assemble and bake you will also need:

1 bowl with salted warm water to seal the empanadas

Egg wash (1 egg yolk beaten with 1 teaspoon water) to brush

Vegetable oil for brushing baking sheet or parchment paper

Heat the vegetable shortening or oil in a large pot over medium heat. Add the chopped white parts of the scallions, onions, paprika, and green pepper and sauté. When the vegetable mix is soft (about 10 minutes), add the tomato paste and tomatoes and stir. Add the flaked tuna, salt, pepper, green part of the scallions, olives and dill. Set aside to cool. Leave the tuna filling covered in the refrigerator overnight or longer, up to two days.

When you are ready to make the empanadas, put about 2 to 3 tablespoons of the filling and a piece of hard-boiled egg in the center of a 4½- to 5½-inch dough disk (see Chapter I for dough recipes). Brush half of the dough edge with warm water, fold it over the filling, press

it with your fingers, then make the *repulgue* (see Chapter II for options). Repeat with the remaining filling. Brush the empanadas with the egg wash.

Brush an oven tray with a film of canola (or other vegetable oil) and put the tray in a 400 degree preheated oven. When the oil is hot (about 3 minutes) take the tray out and place the empanadas on the tray an inch apart. (Putting the empanadas on a hot oiled sheet ensures a crisp base.) Alternatively, you can place the empanadas on a parchment paper lined baking sheet. Bake for 25 to 30 minutes or until golden brown.

Ready to dip? Try ginger mayonnaise–just mix ¼ cup of mayonnaise with ½ tablespoon of lemon juice, ½ teaspoon of grated fresh ginger, salt and pepper. See Chapter VII for other yogurt-based sauces.

Salmon

Makes enough filling for 24 empanadas

1 medium red pepper, chopped

5 scallions, finely chopped

2 stalks celery finely chopped

2 cloves garlic, chopped

2 teaspoons Dijon mustard

1 teaspoon sweet or smoked paprika

3 tablespoons fresh lemon juice

2 teaspoons dry dill (or 1 heaping tablespoon of chopped fresh dill)

4 oz. cream cheese, room temperature

1 pound flaked, cooked salmon (see note)

¾ teaspoon salt (or more to taste)

½ teaspoon ground pepper (or more to taste)

When ready to assemble and bake you will also need:

1 bowl with salted warm water to seal the empanadas

Egg wash (1 egg yolk beaten with 1 teaspoon water) to brush

Vegetable oil for brushing baking sheet or parchment paper

Combine the red pepper, scallions, celery, and garlic in a bowl. Add the mustard, paprika, lemon juice, dill, and the softened cream cheese. Gently fold in the cooked salmon, salt and pepper. Leave the salmon filling covered in the refrigerator overnight or longer, up to two days.

When ready to make the empanadas, put about 2 to 3 tablespoons of the filling in the center of a 4½- to 5½-inch dough disk (see Chapter I for dough recipes). Brush half of the dough edge with warm water, fold over the filling, press it with your fingers, seal and then make the *repulgue* (see Chapter II for options). Repeat with the remaining filling. Brush the empanadas with the egg wash.

Brush an oven tray with a film of canola (or other vegetable oil) and put the tray in a 400 degree preheated oven. When the oil is hot (about 3 minutes) take the tray out and place the empanadas on the tray an inch apart. (Putting the empanadas on a hot oiled sheet ensures a crisp base.) Alternatively, you can place the empanadas on a parchment paper-lined baking sheet. Bake for 25 to 30 minutes or until golden brown.

NOTE :   This is a great way to use leftover cooked salmon, but you can also use a 15 oz. can of good quality salmon, drained, with skin and bones removed.

Sauces: for salmon empanadas we suggest sour cream and dill, cucumber sauce, or Salsa Verde (Chapter VII).

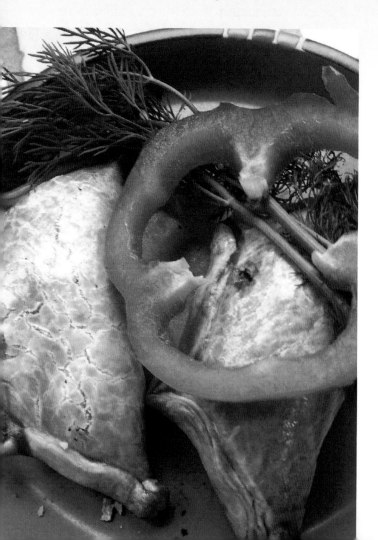

Shrimp

Makes enough filling for 24 empanadas

Note: Using fresh shrimp is the key to this wonderful filling.

¼ cup extra virgin olive oil

2 medium yellow onions, chopped

1 teaspoon sweet or smoked paprika

Pinch of red pepper flakes, or to taste

1 medium green pepper, chopped

1 small red pepper, chopped

3 cloves garlic, chopped

1 pound small fresh shrimp (peeled and deveined), cut in half if desired

¾ teaspoon salt (or more to taste)

½ teaspoon ground pepper (or more to taste)

Pinch of Old Bay seafood seasoning (optional)

½ cup of chopped cilantro or parsley

Squeeze of fresh lemon juice

When ready to assemble and bake you will also need:

1 bowl with salted warm water to seal the empanadas

Egg wash (1 egg yolk beaten with 1 teaspoon water) to brush

Vegetable oil for brushing baking sheet or parchment paper

Heat the oil in a large skillet over medium heat. Add the chopped onions, paprika, pepper flakes and green and red pepper. Sauté over medium heat until soft (about 8 minutes); add the garlic and stir. Add the shrimp and cook until the shrimp turns pink (about 2 minutes). Add the salt and pepper and Old Bay seasoning. Remove from heat and add the cilantro or parsley and the lemon juice. Mix to combine.

Leave the shrimp filling covered in the refrigerator overnight. When ready to make the empanadas, put about 2 to 3 tablespoons of the filling in the center of a 4½- to 5½-inch dough disk (see Chapter I for dough recipes). Brush half of the dough edge with warm water, fold over the filling, press it with your fingers, and then make the *repulgue* (see Chapter II for options). Repeat with the remaining filling. Brush the empanadas with the egg wash.

Brush an oven tray with a film of canola (or other vegetable oil) and put the tray in a 400 degree preheated oven. When the oil is hot take the tray out and place the empanadas on the tray an inch apart. (Putting the empanadas on a hot oiled sheet ensures a crispy base.) Alternatively, you can place the empanadas on a parchment paper-lined baking sheet. Bake for 25 to 30 minutes or until golden brown.

Go-withs might include soy sauce and grated ginger, pineapple salsa, or mango salsa (Chapter VII).

CHAPTER V

Vegetable, Cheese, and Egg Fillings

Spinach

Makes enough filling for 24 empanadas

2 tablespoons vegetable oil

2 tablespoons unsalted butter

2 medium yellow onions, thinly sliced

1 clove garlic, crushed

2 tablespoons flour

3 oz. cream cheese, cut into pieces

2 cups cooked fresh spinach or 15 oz. frozen spinach defrosted, fully drained and moisture squeezed out

½ teaspoon grated nutmeg

¾ teaspoon salt (or more to taste)

¾ teaspoon ground pepper (or more to taste)

2 hard-boiled eggs, coarsely chopped (optional)

1 cup good quality mozzarella, grated, or 1 cup cubed fresh mozzarella

When ready to assemble and bake you will also need:

1 bowl with salted warm water to seal the empanadas

Egg wash (1 egg yolk beaten with 1 teaspoon water) to brush

Vegetable oil for brushing baking sheet or parchment paper

Heat the oil and butter in a large skillet over medium heat. Add the onions and sauté for 8 minutes until soft, stirring a few times. Add the garlic and cook for another minute. Add the flour, stir for a minute and then add the cream cheese. Cook for 5 minutes, stirring, until the cream cheese has melted. Add the drained spinach, nutmeg, salt and pepper, and mix to combine. Set aside. Leave the spinach filling covered in the refrigerator overnight or longer, up to two days.

When ready to make the empanadas, put about 2 tablespoons of the spinach filling, a couple of pieces of the chopped hard-boiled egg, and three small cubes of mozzarella cheese (or 1 teaspoon of grated cheese) in the center of a 4½- to 5½-inch dough disk (see Chapter I for dough recipes). Brush half of the dough edge with warm water, fold it over the filling, press it with your fingers to seal, and make the *repulgue* (see Chapter II for options). Repeat with the remaining filling. Brush the empanadas with the egg wash.

Brush an oven tray with a film of canola (or other vegetable oil) and put the tray in a 400 degree preheated oven. When the oil is hot (around 3 minutes) take the tray out and place the empanadas on the tray an inch apart. (Putting the empanadas on a hot oiled sheet ensures a crispy base.) Alternatively, you can place the empanadas on a parchment paper-lined baking sheet. Bake for 25 to 30 minutes or until golden brown.

NOTES: Chopped fresh chard may be substituted for the spinach in this recipe.

Empanadas with this filling can be wrapped well and frozen for future baking, but if adding hard-boiled egg to the filling make sure it is chopped finely or the boiled eggs will loose their chemical integrity.

Humita (Corn)

Makes enough filling for 24 empanadas

2 tablespoons vegetable oil

2 tablespoons unsalted butter

1 medium yellow onion, chopped

1 medium red pepper, chopped

¾ teaspoon red pepper flakes

½ teaspoon smoked paprika

½ tablespoon sugar

2 tablespoons flour

1 15 oz. can cream corn

1 15 oz. can whole kernel corn, drained

½ teaspoon grated nutmeg

½ teaspoon cinnamon

½ teaspoon salt (or more to taste)

½ teaspoon ground pepper (or more to taste)

1 cup cheddar or mozzarella cheese, grated

When ready to assemble and bake you will also need:

1 bowl with salted warm water to seal the empanadas

Egg wash (1 egg yolk beaten with 1 teaspoon water) to brush

Vegetable oil for brushing baking sheet or parchment paper

Heat the oil and butter in a skillet over medium heat. Add the onions, red pepper, red pepper flakes, and smoked paprika; sauté for 8 minutes until the onions are soft, stirring a few times. Add the sugar and flour. Cook, stirring, another 5 minutes and then add the creamed corn and whole kernel corn. Set aside. When the mixture cools, add the nutmeg, cinnamon, salt and pepper. Leave the *humita* filling covered in the refrigerator overnight or longer up to 24 hours.

When ready to make the empanadas, mix in the cheese and put about 2 to 3 tablespoons of the filling mix in the center of a 4½- to 5½-inch dough disk (see Chapter I for dough recipes). Brush half of the dough edge with warm water, fold it over the filling and press it with your fingers to seal, and make the *repulgue* (see Chapter II for options). Repeat with the remaining filling. Brush the empanadas with the egg wash and sprinkle with paprika and sugar.

Brush an oven tray with a film of canola (or other vegetable oil) and put the tray in a 400 degree preheated oven. When the oil is hot (around 3 minutes) take the tray out and place the empanadas on the tray an inch apart. (Putting the empanadas on a hot oiled sheet ensures a crispy base.) Alternatively, you can place the empanadas on a parchment paper-lined baking sheet. Bake for 25 to 30 minutes or until golden brown.

Caramelized Onion
Makes enough filling for 24 empanadas

The beauty of this caramelized onion filling is that the variations are endless. A few suggestions are offered here. Get creative!

2 tablespoons extra virgin olive oil

2 tablespoons unsalted butter

3 large yellow onions, thinly sliced

1 clove garlic, crushed

½ tablespoon sugar

1 teaspoon balsamic vinegar

Ground black pepper and salt to taste

When ready to assemble and bake you will also need:

1 bowl with salted warm water to seal the empanadas

Egg wash (1 egg yolk beaten with 1 teaspoon water) to brush

Vegetable oil for brushing baking sheet or parchment paper

Heat the oil and butter in a skillet over medium heat. Add the onions and cook for 20 minutes until golden brown and caramelized, stirring a few times. Add the garlic, sugar, balsamic vinegar, salt and pepper. Cook for another 5 minutes. Set aside until the mixture cools. Once cool, the onion filling may be used as is, or enhanced with any of the following options. It is also delicious with 2 tablespoons of grated Parmesan cheese.

NOTE: The Argentinean version (called fugazza) calls for coarsely chopped onions (not sliced), no sugar or balsamic vinegar, and less cooking time (10 minutes) along with the addition of two tablespoons of oregano and ground black pepper.

Goat Cheese
Makes enough filling for 12 empanadas

4 oz. goat cheese, crumbled

1½ teaspoons dried herbs such as thyme, dill, or parsley

salt and pepper to taste

2 cups caramelized onion mixture (see recipe above)

Potato
Makes enough filling for 12 empanadas

1½ cups cooked mashed potatoes

salt and ground black pepper to taste (use plenty of pepper)

1 cup caramelized onion mixture (see recipe above)

Blue Cheese and Walnuts
Makes enough filling for 12 empanadas

4 oz. blue cheese, crumbled

8 oz. cream cheese, softened

1 tablespoon whisky or scotch (optional)

½ cup walnuts, chopped

pepper to taste

1 cup caramelized onion mixture (see recipe above)

Fig and Goat Cheese
Makes enough filling for 12 empanadas

4 oz. goat cheese, crumbled

4 oz. fig jam or preserves

a dash of black pepper

½ teaspoon finely chopped fresh rosemary

1½ cups caramelized onion mixture (see recipe above)

Vegetable oil for brushing baking sheet or parchment paper

When ready to make the empanadas, incorporate the caramelized onions with any of the optional variations. Put about 2 to 3 tablespoons of the filling in the center of a 4½- to 5½-inch dough disk (see Chapter I for dough recipes). Brush half of the dough edge with warm water, fold it, press it with your fingers to seal, and then make the "*repulgue*" (see Chapter II for options). Repeat with the remaining filling. Brush the empanadas with the egg wash. Optional: sprinkle with paprika or other dried herb.

Brush an oven tray with a film of canola (or other vegetable oil) and put the tray in a 400 degrees preheated oven. When the oil is hot (around 3 minutes) take the tray out and place the empanadas on the tray an inch apart. (Putting the empanadas on a hot oiled sheet ensures a crispy base.) Alternatively, you can place the empanadas on a parchment paper lined baking sheet. Bake for 25 to 30 minutes or until golden brown.

Mushroom
Makes enough filling for 24 empanadas

2 tablespoons butter

1 tablespoon olive oil

2 medium yellow onions, diced

1 stalk celery, finely chopped

salt and pepper to taste

2 portabella mushrooms, coarsely chopped

4 oz. white mushrooms, coarsely chopped

2 cloves garlic, minced

1 tablespoon flour

2 tablespoons parsley, chopped

½ tablespoon dried basil or 1 tablespoon fresh, chopped

2 tablespoons brandy or Madeira

½ cup grated Parmesan (optional)

When ready to assemble and bake you will also need:

1 bowl with salted warm water to seal the empanadas

Egg wash (1 egg yolk beaten with 1 teaspoon water) to brush

Vegetable oil for brushing baking sheet or parchment paper

Heat the butter and olive oil in a large skillet over medium heat. Add the onions and celery and sauté for about 8 minutes. Add the salt and pepper and chopped mushrooms and cook for 5 minutes, stirring a few times. Add the garlic, flour, parsley, and basil and mix to combine. Cook for about a minute until the flour is incorporated. Stir in the brandy or Madeira and let it cook for a minute or two until the liquid evaporates. Set aside. Leave the filling covered in the refrigerator overnight or longer, for up to 2 days.

When ready to make the empanadas, mix in the cheese (if desired) and put about 2 to 3 tablespoons of the filling mix in the center of a 4½- to 5½-inch dough disk (see Chapter I for dough recipes). Brush half of the dough edge with warm water, fold it over the filling and press it with your fingers to seal,

and then make the *"repulgue"* (see Chapter II for options). Repeat with the remaining filling. Brush the empanadas with the egg wash.

Brush an oven tray with a film of canola (or other vegetable oil) and put the tray in a 400 degrees preheated oven. When the oil is hot (around 3 minutes) take the tray out and place the empanadas on the tray an inch apart. (Putting the empanadas on a hot oiled sheet ensures a crispy base.) Alternatively, you can place the empanadas on a parchment paper lined baking sheet. Bake for 25 to 30 minutes or until golden brown.

Butternut Squash
Makes enough filling for 24 empanadas

1 large butternut squash (about 2 to 3 pounds)

1 Granny Smith apple, peeled, cored, and chopped into ½-inch pieces

1½ tablespoons chopped fresh sage

3 tablespoons apple juice

1 teaspoon curry powder (or to taste)

3 tablespoons crushed amaretti cookies or bread crumbs

salt and pepper to taste

When ready to assemble and bake you will also need:
1 bowl with salted warm water to seal the empanadas

Egg wash (1 egg yolk beaten with 1 teaspoon water) to brush

Vegetable oil for brushing baking sheet or parchment paper

Preheat the oven to 400 degrees. Using a large sharp knife, carefully cut the butternut squash in half vertically. Using a spoon, scoop out the seeds. Prick the skin in several places with a fork, brush all surfaces lightly with oil, sprinkle the cut side with a little salt and place cut side down on a baking sheet. Roast in the oven for 40 to 50 minutes until you can easily pierce the squash with a fork. Remove from the oven and let cool until you can handle it. Peel off the skin using a vegetable peeler or a paring knife, and then chop the flesh into ½-inch pieces. You should have about 3 cups of chopped squash.

Combine the cooked and chopped squash with the chopped apples, fresh sage, apple juice, curry, crushed amaretti cookies, salt and pepper. Mix gently. When ready to make the empanadas, put about 2 to 3 table-spoons of the filling in the center of a 4½- to 5½-inch dough disk (see Chapter I for dough recipes). Brush half of the dough edge with warm water, fold it over the filling, press it with your fingers to seal, then make the "*repulgue*" (see Chapter II for options). Repeat with the remaining filling. Brush the empanadas with the egg wash.

Brush an oven tray with a film of canola (or other vegetable oil) and put the tray in a 400 degree preheated oven. When the oil is hot (around 3 minutes) take the tray out and place the empanadas on the tray an inch apart.

(Putting the empanadas on a hot oiled sheet ensures a crispy base.) Alternatively, you can place the empanadas on a parchment paper-lined baking sheet. Bake for 25 to 30 minutes or until golden brown.

VARIATIONS: Replace apples, apple juice, curry and amaretti with 2 leeks (white and half of the green part) finely chopped and sautéed in two tablespoons of butter for 15 minutes at medium heat and 1 cup of grated gruyere cheese.

NOTE: Leeks tend to collect dirt between the leaves. The best way to wash them is to cut the leek in half lengthwise and fan open the leaves while holding under cold running water. Dry them with paper towels and chop them finely discarding the top half of the green section.

Caprese
Makes enough filling for 24 empanadas

4 large tomatoes, seeded, chopped and drained (see directions below)

2½ cups chopped mozzarella cheese

2 cloves garlic, chopped

3 tablespoons grated Parmesan cheese

24 fresh basil leaves cut in fine ribbons

3 tablespoons chopped fresh parsley

1 tablespoon bread crumbs

½ teaspoon dried Italian seasoning or dried oregano

salt and pepper to taste

1 cup whole milk ricotta cheese

When ready to assemble and bake you will also need:

1 bowl with salted warm water to seal the empanadas

Egg wash (1 egg yolk beaten with 1 teaspoon water) to brush

Vegetable oil for brushing baking sheet or parchment paper

Cut the tomatoes into quarters. Remove the inner core and seeds, chop the flesh and place in a strainer for a two or three hours to drain. In a bowl, mix together the mozzarella, garlic, tomatoes, Parmesan cheese, basil and parsley. Add the bread crumbs, dried oregano, chopped garlic, salt, and pepper and mix to combine.

When ready to make the empanadas, put 1 tablespoon of ricotta cheese and 2 tablespoons of the filling in the center of a 4½- to 5½-inch dough disk (see Chapter I for dough recipes). Brush half of the dough edge with warm water, fold it over, press it with your fingers to seal, then make the "*repulgue*" (see Chapter II for options). Repeat with the remaining filling. Brush the empanadas with the egg wash and sprinkle with black pepper.

Brush an oven tray with a film of canola (or other vegetable oil) and put the tray in a 400 degree preheated oven. When the oil is hot (around 3 minutes) take the tray out and place the empanadas on the tray an inch apart. (Putting the empanadas on a hot oiled sheet ensures a crispy base.) Alternatively, you can place the empanadas on a parchment paper-lined baking sheet. Bake for 25 to 30 minutes or until golden brown.

Garden Patch
Makes enough filling for 24 empanadas

Leftover cooked vegetables would work beautifully in this recipe.

2 tablespoons extra virgin olive oil

1 tablespoon unsalted butter

1 large yellow onion, chopped

1 red bell pepper, chopped

4 oz. button mushrooms, chopped

2 cloves garlic, minced

1 cup frozen peas (unthawed)

1 small can (4 oz.) of chopped tomatoes, drained

1 tablespoon dried oregano

1 teaspoon chili powder

1 teaspoon curry powder

½ teaspoon smoked paprika

1 teaspoon honey

1 teaspoon salt and ½ teaspoon pepper, or to taste

2 tablespoons flour mixed with ¼ cup of cold water until a smooth paste is formed

2 medium potatoes, boiled and cut into cooked small cubes

2 small carrots, cooked and cut in half moon slices

When ready to assemble and bake you will also need:

1 bowl with salted warm water to seal the empanadas

Egg wash (1 egg yolk beaten with 1 teaspoon water) to brush

Vegetable oil for brushing baking sheet or parchment paper

Heat the butter and olive oil in a large skillet over medium heat. Add the onion and red pepper and cook for 5 minutes. Add the chopped mushrooms and garlic and cook for 5 minutes, stirring a few times. Then add the frozen peas and tomatoes and mix; when heated through, add the oregano, chili powder, curry powder, paprika, honey, salt and pepper. Incorporate the flour slurry and cook, stirring constantly, for two minutes until it thickens. Finally add the carrots and potatoes. Set aside to cool. Leave the filling covered in the refrigerator overnight or longer, up to 2 days.

When ready to make the empanadas put 2 to 3 tablespoons of the filling in the center of a 4½- to 5½-inch dough disk (see Chapter I for dough recipes). Brush half of the dough edge with warm water, fold it, press it with your fingers to seal, then make the "*repulgue*" (see Chapter II for options). Repeat with the remaining filling. Brush the empanadas with the egg wash.

Brush an oven tray with a film of canola (or other vegetable oil) and put the tray in a 400 degree preheated oven. When the oil is hot (around 3 minutes) take the tray out and place the empanadas on the tray an inch apart. (Putting the empanadas on a hot oiled sheet ensures a crispy base.) Alternatively, you can place the empanadas on a parchment paper lined baking sheet. Bake for 25 to 30 minutes or until golden brown.

NOTE: A nice sauce to serve with these empanadas would be yogurt or sour cream mixed with fresh mint and ground black pepper (Chapter VII).

Potato
Makes enough filling for 24 empanadas

3 tablespoons vegetable oil

2 large yellow onions, chopped

2 cloves garlic, chopped

4 large potatoes, cooked and cut into small cubes

1 teaspoon chili powder

1 teaspoon cumin powder

salt and pepper to taste

1 cup grated cheddar or Monterrey Jack cheese

When ready to assemble and bake you will also need:

1 bowl with salted warm water to seal the empanadas

Egg wash (1 egg yolk beaten with 1 teaspoon water) to brush

Vegetable oil for brushing baking sheet or parchment paper

Heat the oil in a skillet over medium heat. Add the onion and cook for 8 minutes until it is transparent. Add the garlic and cook for another minute. Add the cooked potatoes and mix well; cook and stir for a few minutes. Add the chili powder, cumin, salt and pepper. Remove from heat and set aside. Leave the filling covered in the refrigerator overnight or longer, up to 2 days.

When ready to make the empanadas mix in the grated cheese and put 2 to 3 tablespoons of the potato filling in the center of a 4½- to 5½-inch dough disk (see Chapter I for dough recipes). Brush half of the dough edge with warm water, fold it, press it with your fingers to seal, and then make the "*repulgue*" (see Chapter II for options). Repeat with the remaining filling. Brush the empanadas with the egg wash.

Brush an oven tray with a film of canola (or other vegetable oil) and put the tray in a 400 degree preheated oven. When the oil is hot (around 3 minutes) take the tray out and place the empanadas on the tray an inch apart. (Putting the empanadas on a hot oiled sheet ensures a crispy base.) Alternatively, you can place the empanadas on a parchment paper-lined baking sheet. Bake for 25 to 30 minutes or until golden brown.

Black Beans with Jalapeño
Makes enough filling for 24 empanadas

2 tablespoons extra virgin olive oil

1 large red onion, chopped

3 cloves garlic, chopped

1 large potato, finely diced

2 small carrots, grated or diced

2½ teaspoons dried oregano

1½ teaspoons ground cumin

1 jalapeño pepper, seeded, veins removed, and diced (½ to 1 whole pepper, depending on desired heat)

2 cans black beans, drained and rinsed and coarsely mashed

salt and pepper to taste

juice of 1 lime

¾ cup jarred Mexican salsa, medium or mild

1½ cups grated Monterrey Jack or cheddar cheese

When ready to assemble and bake you will also need:

1 bowl with salted warm water to seal the empanadas

Egg wash (1 egg yolk beaten with 1 teaspoon water) to brush

Vegetable oil for brushing baking sheet or parchment paper

Heat the oil and add the onions. Cook until soft, about 7 minutes. Add the garlic and cook for a minute. Add the potato and carrots. Cook until the vegetables are soft, stirring occasionally. Add in the oregano, cumin, and jalapeño pepper. Incorporate the black beans and mix to combine. Season with salt and pepper. Add the lime juice and salsa. Mix to combine. Set aside. Leave the mix covered in the refrigerator overnight or longer, up to 2 days.

When ready to make the empanadas mix in the grated cheese and put 2 to 3 tablespoons of the black bean filling in the center of a 4½- to 5½-inch dough disk (see Chapter I for dough recipes). Brush half of the dough edge with warm water, fold it over the filling, press it with your fingers to seal, then make the *"repulgue"* (see Chapter II for options). Repeat with the remaining filling. Brush the empanadas with the egg wash.

Brush an oven tray with a film of canola (or other vegetable oil) and put the tray in a 400 degree preheated oven. When the oil is hot (around 3 minutes) take the tray out and place the empanadas on the tray an inch apart. (Putting the empanadas on a hot oiled sheet ensures a crispy base.) Alternatively, you can place the empanadas on a parchment paper-lined baking sheet. Bake for 25 to 30 minutes or until golden brown.

NOTE: If you want a dipping sauce, salsas are the best companions!

Tofu

Makes enough filling for 24 empanadas

2 tablespoons olive oil

½ teaspoon red pepper flakes

2 red bell peppers, chopped

1 small onion, thinly sliced

4 cloves garlic, chopped

16 oz. medium or firm tofu, cut into small cubes

6 scallions, chopped

2 cups cooked rice (white or brown)

2 cups chopped fresh spinach leaves

1 teaspoon curry powder, or to taste

salt and pepper to taste

When ready to assemble and bake you will also need:

1 bowl with salted warm water to seal the empanadas

Egg wash (1 egg yolk beaten with 1 teaspoon water) to brush

Vegetable oil for brushing baking sheet or parchment paper

Heat the oil and add red pepper flakes and the red bell peppers and onions. Cook until soft, about 8 minutes. Add the garlic and cook for a minute. Add the tofu, scallions and rice and mix to combine. Incorporate the spinach. Mix to combine and cook for one minute. Add curry powder and, salt and pepper. Remove from heat and set aside. Leave the mix covered in the refrigerator overnight or longer, up to 2 days.

When ready to make the empanadas put 2 to 3 tablespoons of the tofu filling in the center of a 4½- to 5½- inch dough disk (see Chapter I for dough recipes). Brush half of the dough edge with warm water, fold it over the filling, press it with your fingers to seal, then make the "*repulgue*" (see Chapter II for options). Repeat with the remaining filling. Brush the empanadas with the egg wash.

Brush an oven tray with a film of canola (or other vegetable oil) and put the tray in a 400 degree preheated oven. When the oil is hot (around 3 minutes) take the tray out and place the empanadas on the tray an inch apart. (Putting the empanadas on a hot oiled sheet ensures a crispy base.) Alternatively, you can place the empanadas on a parchment paper-lined baking sheet. Bake for 25 to 30 minutes or until golden brown.

NOTE: These are delicious served with yogurt sauce (Chapter VII), black bean dip, or salsa.

Eggs

Makes enough filling for 24 empanadas

3 tablespoons olive oil

2 large yellow onions, chopped

2 cloves of garlic, chopped

3 tablespoons roasted green or red chile

4 strips of cooked bacon or 4 sausage links, chopped (optional)

3 medium or 2 large potatoes, cooked, cooled, and cut into small cubes

12 large eggs

1 cup grated cheddar or Monterrey Jack or pepper jack cheese

salt and pepper to taste

When ready to assemble and bake you will also need:

1 bowl with salted warm water to seal the empanadas

Egg wash (1 egg yolk beaten with 1 teaspoon water) to brush

Vegetable oil for brushing baking sheet or parchment paper

Heat the oil in a large skillet and add onions. Cook on medium heat, stirring occasionally, until soft, about 7 minutes. Add the garlic and green or red chili; cook for a minute. Add the sausage or bacon and mix to combine. Incorporate the potatoes and cook for a few minutes until the potatoes have some color.

In a separate bowl whisk the eggs. Incorporate the egg mixture into the skillet and stir until the eggs start to set but are not dry. Stir in the cheese and mix well. Add salt and pepper. Set aside to cool a bit.

When ready to make the empanadas put 2 to 3 tablespoons of the egg filling in the center of a 4½- to 5½- inch dough disk (see Chapter I for dough recipes). Brush half of the dough edge with warm water, fold it over the filling, press it with your fingers to seal, then make the *"repulgue"* (see Chapter II for options). Repeat with the remaining filling. Brush the empanadas with the egg wash.

Brush an oven tray with a film of canola (or other vegetable oil) and put the tray in a 400 degrees preheated oven. When the oil is hot (around 3 minutes) take the tray out and place the empanadas on the tray an inch apart. (Putting the empanadas on a hot oiled sheet ensures a crispy base.) Alternatively, you can place the empanadas on a parchment paper-lined baking sheet. Bake for 25 to 30 minutes or until golden brown.

NOTE: Turkey bacon or sausage may be substituted.

Serve with any prepared tomato or chile salsa.

Chapter VI

Sweet Dessert Empanadas

Caramel Apple

Makes enough filling for 24 empanadas

2 tablespoons unsalted butter

4 or 5 Granny Smith apples, peeled, cored, and cut into ½-inch pieces

½ cup sugar

1 to 2 teaspoons cinnamon

¼ cup packed brown sugar

Pinch of salt

Pinch of ground nutmeg

2 tablespoons cornstarch

3 tablespoon prepared caramel sauce or dulce de leche

When ready to assemble and bake you will also need:

1 egg yolk plus 1 tablespoon milk or half and half for brushing the dough

Cinnamon sugar or flaked sea salt for sprinkling

Parchment paper

Put the cubed apples in a saucepan with the butter, sugar, cinnamon, brown sugar, salt, and nutmeg. Stir the apples over medium heat, cooking them until they are just tender but not mushy, about 8 minutes. In a small bowl, mix the corn starch with 2 tablespoons of water and stir until smooth. Add the cornstarch mixture to the apples and cook, stirring, until the mixture starts to thicken, about 1 minute. Remove the pan from the heat and stir in the caramel sauce or dulce de leche, stirring to coat the apples. Chill the apple mixture for at least an hour.

To assemble, spoon about 2 tablespoons of apple filling in the center of each dough round (see Chapter I for pastry dough recipes). Lightly brush around the edges of the dough circle with water. Fold the circle in half, enclosing the filling, and pinch the edges together firmly to seal. Use a fork to crimp and seal all around the edges. Beat the egg yolk with the milk and brush over the empanada. Sprinkle with cinnamon sugar or sea salt. Repeat with the remaining filling.

Line two baking sheets with parchment paper. Place the filled empanadas on the baking sheets, leaving 1 inch between each empanada. Bake in a preheated 350 degree oven for 22 to 28 minutes, or until golden brown. Let cool for 5 minutes, and then transfer to a wire rack to continue cooling.

NOTE: These empanadas are delicious served warm with a sprinkling of powdered sugar and a scoop of vanilla or caramel ice cream, or a dollop of dulce de leche on the side (see Chapter VII).

VARIATIONS: Add 3 tablespoons of dried cranberries or dried cherries to the apple mixture.

Pumpkin

Makes enough filling for 24 empanadas.

This simple but delicious recipe was originally handed down from Tommy Alcala's grandmother, Hortencia Flores. She was famous for her "Abuelita's Empanadas."

1 small can (14 ounces) pure canned pumpkin (not pumpkin pie filling)

¾ cup sugar

1½ teaspoons ground cinnamon

1½ teaspoons ground cloves

When ready to assemble and bake you will also need:

1 egg yolk plus 1 tablespoon of milk or half and half for brushing the dough

Cinnamon-sugar for sprinkling

Parchment paper

Combine all the ingredients in a bowl, and mix well.

To assemble, spoon about 2 tablespoons of pumpkin filling in the center of each dough round (see Chapter I for pastry dough recipes). Lightly brush around the edges of the dough circle with water. Fold the circle in half, enclosing the filling, and pinch the edges together firmly to seal. Use a fork to crimp and seal all around the edges. Beat the egg yolk with the milk and brush over the empanada. Sprinkle with cinnamon sugar. Repeat with the remaining filling.

Line two baking sheets with parchment paper. Place the filled empanadas on the baking sheets, leaving 1 inch between each empanada. Bake in a preheated 350 degree oven for 22 to 28 minutes, or until golden brown. Let cool for 5 minutes, and then transfer to a wire rack to continue cooling. Serve warm, drizzled with maple glaze (recipe below).

VARIATION: Add ¾ cup toasted chopped pecans to the pumpkin filling.

Maple glaze: combine 2 teaspoons pure maple syrup, 1 cup powdered sugar, and 2 tablespoons milk. Stir until combined and smooth. Drizzle over pumpkin empanadas.

Peach Blueberry

Makes enough filling for 24 empanadas.

1 teaspoon cornstarch

1 teaspoon fresh lemon juice

2 ripe peaches, peeled, halved, pitted, and cut into ½-inch pieces

1 tablespoon unsalted butter

1 tablespoon packed brown sugar

Pinch of salt

½ cup fresh blueberries, rinsed

½ teaspoon pure almond extract

When ready to assemble and bake you will also need:

Egg wash (1 egg yolk beaten with 1 tablespoon milk or water) to brush the dough

Sugar for sprinkling (optional)

Parchment paper

Stir together the cornstarch and lemon juice in a small bowl until smooth and the cornstarch is dissolved. Set aside. In a skillet over medium-low heat, melt the butter and add the peaches, brown sugar, and salt, stirring until the sugar dissolves, about 2 minutes. Gently stir in the blueberries. Stir in the cornstarch mixture and bring to a boil. Boil about 1 minute, or until the peaches are tender. Remove from heat. Stir in the almond extract and stir to coat the peaches. Set aside to cool before filling empanadas.

To assemble, spoon about 2 tablespoons of the filling in the center of each dough circle (see Chapter I for pastry dough recipes). Lightly brush around the edges of the dough circle with water. Fold the circle in half, enclosing the filling, and pinch the edges together firmly to seal. Use a fork to

crimp and seal all around the edges. Beat the egg yolk with the milk and brush over the empanada. Sprinkle with sugar, if desired. Repeat with the remaining filling. Cut a small vent in the top.

Line two baking sheets with parchment paper. Place the filled empanadas on the baking sheets, leaving 1 inch between each empanada. Bake in a preheated 350 degree oven for 22 to 28 minutes, or until golden brown. Let cool for 5 minutes, and then transfer to a wire rack to continue cooling. Serve warm.

NOTE: Delicious served warm with a scoop of vanilla ice cream!

Strawberry Rhubarb

Makes enough filling for 24 empanadas

> 4 stalks fresh rhubarb, trimmed and cut into ½-inch pieces
>
> 2 pints fresh strawberries, stemmed and quartered
>
> 2 tablespoons unsalted butter
>
> 6 to 8 tablespoons sugar (or to taste, depending on sweetness of fruit)

> 2 tablespoons flour
>
> 1 teaspoon freshly grated orange zest
>
> 2 tablespoons fresh orange juice
>
> pinch of salt

When ready to assemble and bake you will also need:

> Egg wash (1 egg yolk beaten with 1 tablespoon milk or water) to brush the dough
>
> Sugar for sprinkling (optional)
>
> Parchment paper

Melt the butter in a small skillet over low heat. Add the rhubarb pieces and cook, stirring, about 8 minutes, or until the rhubarb is

soft and tender. Remove from the heat. Add the remaining ingredients, and stir until well blended. Let cool completely before filling empanadas.

To assemble, spoon about 2 tablespoons of the filling in the center of each dough circle (see Chapter I for pastry dough recipes). Lightly brush around the edges of the dough circle with water. Fold the circle in half, enclosing the filling, and pinch the edges together firmly to seal. Use a fork to crimp and seal all around the edges. Beat the egg yolk with the milk and brush over the empanadas. Sprinkle with sugar, if desired. Repeat with the remaining filling. Cut a small vent on the top.

Line two baking sheets with parchment paper. Place the filled empanadas on the baking sheets, leaving 1 inch between each empanada. Bake in a preheated 350 degree oven for 22 to 28 minutes, or until golden brown. Let cool for 5 minutes, and then transfer to a wire rack to continue cooling. Serve warm.

NOTE: Good served with a side of Chantilly cream, ice cream, or simply dusted with confectioner's sugar.

Chocolate Hazelnut Spread or Dulce de Leche and Banana
Makes enough filling for 24 empanadas

12 oz. chocolate hazelnut spread or 12 oz. dulce de leche (or prepared caramel sauce)

3 firm bananas, cut in half-moon slices

When ready to assemble and bake you will also need:

Egg wash for brushing empanadas (1 egg yolk beaten with 1 tablespoon milk or water)

Parchment paper

Spread 1 heaping tablespoon of hazelnut spread or dulce de leche onto half of each pastry circle. Top with three slices of banana in the center of each dough circle (see

Chapter I for pastry dough recipes). Lightly brush around the edges of the dough circle with water. Fold the circle in half, enclosing the filling, and pinch the edges together firmly to seal. Use a fork to crimp and seal all around the edges. Beat the egg yolk with the milk and brush over the empanada. Repeat with the remaining filling.

Line two baking sheets with parchment paper. Place the filled empanadas on the baking sheets, leaving 1 inch between each empanada. Bake in a preheated 350 degree oven for 22 to 28 minutes, or until golden brown. Let cool for 5 minutes, and then transfer to a wire rack to continue cooling. Serve warm.

Chocolate Raspberry
Makes enough filling for 24 empanadas

> 16 ounces bittersweet or semisweet good quality chocolate
>
> 2 cups heavy cream or whipping cream
>
> ¾ cup good quality raspberry jam

When ready to assemble and bake you will also need:
> Egg wash (1 egg yolk beaten with 1 tablespoon of milk) for brushing the dough

Parchment paper

Using a serrated knife, finely chop the chocolate into ¼-inch pieces. Chop thoroughly—large chunks of chocolate will not melt evenly. Place the chopped chocolate in a medium heatproof bowl. Bring the cream to a boil in a small saucepan over medium heat—until the cream really boils and threatens to rise up and boil over the sides.

Remove the pan from the heat and immediately pour over the chopped chocolate. Tap the bowl on the counter to let the cream settle into the chocolate, and then let it sit for 1 minute. With a spatula, slowly stir in a circular motion, being careful not to add too much air to the ganache. Stir until all the chocolate is melted, about 2 minutes. It may look done after one minute, but keep going to make sure it's completely emulsified. This is a basic ganache. Chill the ganache for at least 2 hours before assembling empanadas. Any leftover ganache can be stored covered in the refrigerator for up to two weeks.

When ready to assemble, spread ½ tablespoon of raspberry jam onto half of the pastry circle. Top with a large spoonful of ganache in the center of each dough circle (see Chapter I for pastry dough recipes). Lightly brush around the edges of the dough circle with water. Fold the circle in half, enclosing the filling, and pinch the edges together firmly to seal. Use a fork to crimp and seal all around the edges. Beat the egg yolk with the milk and brush over the empanada. Repeat with the remaining filling.

Line two baking sheets with parchment paper. Place the filled empanadas on the baking sheets, leaving 1 inch between each empanada. Bake in a preheated 350 degree oven for 22 to 28 minutes, or until golden brown. Let cool for 5 minutes, and then transfer to a wire rack to continue cooling. Serve warm.

NOTE: Instead of raspberry jam, you can use orange marmalade and add a bit of grated orange zest to the ganache. Cherry preserves are also delicious.

Pear Almond
Makes enough filling for 24 empanadas

4 teaspoons fresh lemon juice

5 teaspoons cornstarch

2 tablespoons unsalted butter

4 or 5 ripe Bosc pears, peeled

1/3 cup packed brown sugar

1 teaspoon grated lemon zest

Pinch of salt

½ teaspoon pure almond extract

8 oz. (about 1/2 can) canned almond pastry filling (not almond paste)

When ready to assemble and bake you will also need:

Egg wash (1 egg yolk beaten with 1 tablespoon milk or water) to brush the dough

Parchment paper

Stir together the cornstarch and lemon juice in a small bowl until smooth. Set aside. Melt the butter in a small skillet over medium low heat. Halve the pears, remove the cores and stems, and cut into ½-inch pieces. Add the pears to the skillet, along with the brown sugar, zest, and salt. Cook, stirring, about 5 minutes until the pears are tender. Add the cornstarch mixture to the skillet and bring to a boil. Continue to cook and stir about 1 minute, until the liquid is thickened and the pears are tender. Remove from heat. Add the almond extract and stir to coat the pears. Let cool before filling empanadas.

When ready to assemble, spread ½ tablespoon almond pastry filling onto half of the pastry circle. Top with about 2 tablespoons of pear mixture in the center of each dough circle (see Chapter I for pastry dough recipes). Lightly brush around the edges of the dough circle with water. Fold the circle in half, enclosing the filling, and pinch the edges together firmly to seal. Use a fork to crimp and seal all around the edges. Beat

the egg yolk with the milk and brush over the empanada. Repeat with the remaining filling.

Line two baking sheets with parchment paper. Place the filled empanadas on the baking sheets, leaving 1 inch between each empanada. Bake in a preheated 350 degree oven for 22 to 28 minutes, or until golden brown. Let cool for 5 minutes, and then transfer to a wire rack to continue cooling. Serve warm. NOTE: You can add ½ cup fresh cranberries to the skillet when you add the pears. Replace the almond extract with vanilla extract and omit the almond filling.

You may want to serve with a dollop of chocolate sauce or dulce de leche (Chapter VII).

Cherry
Makes enough filling for 24 empanadas

16 oz. frozen pitted sweet cherries, unthawed (or 2 cups pitted fresh cherries)

1½ tablespoons cornstarch

²/₃ cup dried cherries

½ cup sugar

1 teaspoon pure almond extract

Pinch of salt

When ready to assemble and bake you will also need:

Egg wash (1 egg yolk beaten with 1 table-spoon milk or water) to brush the dough

Sugar for sprinkling (optional)

Parchment paper

In a small bowl, combine the cornstarch with 1½ tablespoons cold water and stir until well blended. Combine both kinds of cherries, sugar, extract, and salt in a large saucepan, and cook over medium heat, stirring, until the cherries give off their juices, about 5 minutes. Add the water and cornstarch mixture and bring to a boil, stirring often. Remove from heat and let cool to room tempera-ture, stirring occasionally. Chill for at least 2 hours before assembling.

To assemble, spoon about 2 table-spoons of cherry filling in the center of each dough circle (see Chapter I for pas-try dough recipes). Lightly brush around the edges of the dough circle with water.

Fold the circle in half, enclosing the filling, and pinch the edges together firmly to seal. Use a fork to crimp and seal all around the edges. Brush each empanada with egg wash and cut a small vent on the top. Repeat with the remaining filling. Chill for 30 minutes.

Line two baking sheets with parchment paper. Place the filled empanadas on the baking sheets, leaving 1 inch between each empanada. Bake in a preheated 350 degree oven for 22 to 28 minutes, or until golden brown. Let cool for 5 minutes, and then transfer to a wire rack to continue cooling. Serve warm.

NOTE: You may sprinkle the tops of the egg-washed empanadas with sugar. These are delicious served warm with vanilla ice cream!

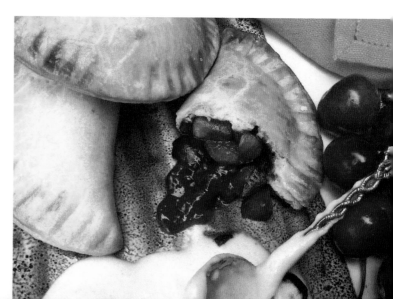

Apricot

Makes enough filling for 24 empanadas

16 oz. dried apricots

1½ cups water

²/₃ cup sugar

¼ teaspoon cinnamon

¾ cup good quality apricot preserves (not jelly)

When ready to assemble and bake you will also need:

Egg wash (1 egg yolk beaten with 1 table-spoon milk or water) to brush the dough

Cinnamon-sugar for sprinkling

Parchment paper

Cut dried apricots into small pieces about ¼ inch dice. In a medium saucepan, combine the apricots and water. Bring to a boil. Cover, reduce the heat to low, and simmer for 15 to 20 minutes. Stir in the sugar and cinnamon and return to a boil. Cover, reduce the heat, and simmer another 10 minutes until most of the water is absorbed and the mixture is very thick. It will thicken more as it cools. Remove

from heat and stir in the apricot preserves. Mix well and refrigerate several hours before assembling empanadas.

To assemble, spoon about 2 tablespoons of the apricot filling in the center of each dough circle (see Chapter I for pastry dough recipes).   Lightly brush around the edges of the dough circle with water. Fold the circle in half, enclosing the filling, and pinch the edges together firmly to seal. Use a fork to crimp and seal all around the edges. Beat the egg yolk with the milk and brush over the empanada. Repeat with the remaining filling. Sprinkle empanadas with cinnamon sugar, if desired.

Line two baking sheets with parchment paper. Place the filled empanadas on the baking sheets, leaving 1 inch between each

empanada. Bake in a preheated 350 degree oven for 22 to 28 minutes, or until golden brown. Let cool for 5 minutes, and then transfer to a wire rack to continue cooling. Serve warm.

NOTE: These empanadas are delicious served with a drizzle of chocolate sauce (see Chapter VII).

Guava or Quince (Membrillo)
Makes enough filling for 24 empanadas

12 oz. cream cheese, softened (or 12 oz. whole milk ricotta cheese)

1½ cups sweet creamed guava or quince, diced (or quince paste)

When ready to assemble and bake you will also need:

1 egg yolk mixed with 1 tablespoon milk or water to brush the empanadas

Parchment paper

Mix the cream cheese and guava or quince until combined. Place about 2 tablespoons of the guava or quince filling onto half of the pastry circle (see Chapter I for pastry dough recipes). Lightly brush around the edges of the dough circle with water. Fold the circle in half, enclosing the filling, and pinch the edges together firmly to seal. Use a fork to crimp and seal all around the edges. Beat the egg yolk with the milk and brush over the empanada. Repeat with the remaining filling.

Line two baking sheets with parchment paper. Place the filled empanadas on the baking sheets, leaving 1 inch between each empanada. Bake in a preheated 350 degree oven for 22 to 28 minutes, or until golden brown. Let cool for 5 minutes, and then transfer to a wire rack to continue cooling. Serve warm.

NOTE: creamed guava, creamed quince, and quince paste may be found in Latin American markets.

CHAPTER VII

Sauces, Salsas, and Accompaniments

Chimichurri

Makes about 2 cups of sauce

$1/3$ cup dried oregano

1½ tablespoons crushed red pepper

2 bay leaves, crushed

1 teaspoon cumin

1 teaspoon paprika

10 garlic cloves, minced

1½ cups warm water

½ cup vegetable oil

½ cup red wine vinegar or ¼ cup red wine and ¼ cup red wine vinegar

Kosher salt and pepper

$1/3$ cup chopped fresh parsley

2 scallions, finely chopped

½ yellow onion, finely chopped

Mix all the dry ingredients, the garlic and the warm water in a large jar and shake well to combine. Let it stand for half an hour at room temperature. Add the oil, vinegar, wine, salt and pepper. Shake again. Add the fresh herbs and onions. Shake to combine. Chill at least 12 hours or more in the refrigerator to allow flavors to develop, shaking it occasionally before using. Store in the refrigerator for up to one week.

NOTE: Chimichurri lasts for a long time, especially if it is made only with dry ingredients. Replace the fresh parsley with other dry herbs such as dry basil or dry parsley and use dehydrated onions instead of fresh onions. Store in the refrigerator up to a month. The flavor of chimichurri improves with time!

Salsa Verde
Makes one cup

¾ cup Italian parsley

4 garlic cloves, chopped

1 teaspoon cumin

1/3 cup parsley, chopped

3 scallions, chopped

½ cup olive oil

½ teaspoon fresh lemon juice

2 tablespoons drained capers

salt and pepper to taste

Put all the ingredients in a food processor and pulse several times. Do not over-process. Pour into a jar and chill. This sauce can be refrigerated up to a week. Serve at room temperature.

Fruit Salsa (Pineapple or Mango)
Makes 1½ cups

1 cup fresh pineapple or mango (finely chopped)

½ cup chopped red bell pepper

½ cup chopped scallions

½ cup chopped fresh cilantro

¼ cup orange or lime juice, freshly squeezed

2 green chili peppers or jalapeños, finely chopped

1 clove garlic, finely chopped

1 tablespoon extra virgin olive oil

salt and pepper to taste

- 1 teaspoon curry powder mixed with a large pinch of salt
- 1 teaspoon fresh grated ginger + 1 minced scallion + salt and pepper
- 1 teaspoon grated lemon peel, 1 teaspoon dried thyme, 1 teaspoon cracked black pepper, and 1 tablespoon chopped fresh parsley
- 2 tablespoons chopped sun dried tomatoes in oil, 1 tablespoon minced Calamata olives, and 1 garlic clove minced
- 1½ teaspoons grated lime peel, 2 teaspoons minced jalapeño, 1 tablespoon chopped cilantro, and ½ teaspoon cumin
- 1 teaspoon whole grain or English mustard, 1 teaspoon dry dill, 1 teaspoon lemon juice, and salt pepper

Mix all the ingredients together and refrigerate. Salsa can be made a day ahead, but do not add the fruit juice until just before serving.

Yogurt or Sour Cream with Spices
Makes 1 cup

8 oz. plain Greek yogurt or sour cream (or a combination of both)

Add one of the following and mix until blended:

Dulce de Leche Sauce

Makes 4 cups

Store the dulce de leche in a sterilized glass jar in the refrigerator for up to a year!

2 quarts whole milk

2 cups (I pound) sugar

1 teaspoon baking soda

1 vanilla bean

In a heavy non-stick saucepan over medium heat, add the milk, sugar, and vanilla bean, stirring until the sugar is dissolved. Bring to a boil and add the baking soda while stirring. Reduce the heat to low and stir occasionally with a wooden spoon or heatproof spatula.

Once the mixture starts to thicken, stir regularly. Cook for two to three hours over low heat, stirring often. The sauce is finished when the color is a rich caramel brown and very thick. To test, drop a spoonful of the sauce onto a plate and allow to cool for a few minutes. Tilt the plate; if the sauce doesn't run, it is ready. Remove and discard the vanilla bean and cool the mixture before refrigerating.

An alternative method uses canned sweetened condensed milk. It still requires a three-hour time commitment, but eliminates the need to stir the mixture for that length of time.

1 can (14 oz.) sweetened condensed (not evaporated) milk, unopened, with the label removed

Pierce two or three holes in the top of the can. Place the can upright in a small pot with enough water in the pot to come ¾ of the way up the can. Heat over medium heat uncovered for five minutes. Reduce the heat to low and simmer uncovered for three to three and a half hours, depending on desired thickness. Check the pot occasionally to ensure that the water covers ¾ of the can; add water when needed. At the end of the cooking period, very carefully remove the can from the

water with tongs and allow the can to cool. Once cool, open the can and stir the contents until smooth. Pour the cooled dulce de leche into a jar and refrigerate, covered. The sauce will last up to three weeks in the refrigerator.

NOTE: *canned ready-to-serve dulce de leche caramel sauce may also be found in many Latin American markets, or in the Mexican food section of many supermarkets.*

Chocolate Sauce
Makes 1 cup
Store this chocolate sauce in a covered glass jar in the refrigerator for up to three months.

7½ oz. bittersweet or semisweet chocolate, chopped

½ cup plus 2 tablespoons water

½ cup light corn syrup

¾ cup unsweetened cocoa powder

¼ cup sugar

¾ teaspoon instant coffee granules or ½ teaspoon instant espresso powder

2 tablespoons cognac, brandy, or pure vanilla extract

Melt the chocolate in the microwave or in a double boiler over simmering water. Combine the water, syrup, cocoa, sugar, and coffee in a large saucepan and bring to a boil over medium heat, stirring. Reduce heat and simmer for 2 minutes, stirring constantly to dissolve the sugar and cocoa powder. Whisk in the melted chocolate. Boil for two or three minutes to reduce to the desired consistency. Cool slightly. Whisk in the cognac, brandy, or vanilla extract. Store in a covered glass jar in the refrigerator and reheat before serving.

ABOUT THE AUTHOR

The authors are academics/educators/consultants who decided to devote time to their passion for cooking. They co-own and operate a busy empanadas shop in New Mexico. They have run cooking classes and catered community events – and have travelled extensively in search of the perfect empanada. Their website can be viewed at www.nadabutempanadas.com and on Facebook at https://www.facebook.com/pages/Nada-but-Empanadas/309080492442317

38052374R00052

Made in the USA
Lexington, KY
19 December 2014